THE ONLY PSYCHIC POWER BOOK YOU'LL EVER NEED

Develop Your Innate Ability to Predict the Future

Michael R. Hathaway, D.C.H.

A adamsmedia
Avon, Massachusetts

Published by
Adams Media, an F+W Publications Company
57 Littlefield Street, Avon, MA 02322. U.S.A.

www.adamsmedia.com

ISBN-13: 978-1-59869-551-9
ISBN-10: 1-59869-551-7

Printed in Canada.

Library of Congress Cataloging-in-Publication Data
is available from the publisher.

This publication is designed to provide accurate and authoritative information with
regard to the subject matter covered. It is sold with the understanding that the
publisher is not engaged in rendering legal, accounting, or other professional advice.
If legal advice or other expert assistance is required, the services of a competent
professional person should be sought.

—From a *Declaration of Principles* jointly adopted by a Committee of the American
Bar Association and a Committee of Publishers and Associations

Contains materials adopted and abridged from *The Everything*® *Psychic Book* by
Michael R. Hathaway, D.C.H., Copyright © 2003 by F+W Publications, Inc.

This book is available at quantity discounts for bulk purchases.
For information, please call 1-800-289-0963.

Contents

CHAPTER 4: LOOKING OUT OF YOUR THIRD EYE INTO YOUR CHAKRAS

CHAPTER 5: CLAIRVOYANCE IS A VISUAL GIFT

CHAPTER 6: WHAT ARE YOU HEARING? CLAIRAUDIENCE

Human beings have been attempting to learn the answers to the puzzles of the Universe since the beginning of existence. And today, people are just as interested in the unknown as ever. That's why you've picked up this book!

Many of you want to know what the purpose of life is all about. And you may wonder if you have some sort of psychic ability like Sylvia Browne, John Edward, or James Van Praagh. You may have the feeling that you are missing your life's calling, and you want to get yourself back on track. Maybe there is something gnawing at your insides, but you don't know what to do about finding out what it is, much less how to go about addressing it. It may be that day after day and year after year, you continue to feel you are drifting without a central focus for your life. You may have had an early psychic experience that left you with the feeling of something that has yet to be resolved. That experience may have terrified you, and you live in fear of it happening again.

Whatever your burning questions are, you've come to the right place! With *The Only Psychic Power Book You'll Ever Need,* you may find the answers and perhaps a new beginning to your search for the meaning of life. This is the *only* book you'll need because it will teach you how to open yourself up to lessens of the Universe—lessons that will last a lifetime.

Yes, you do have special psychic abilities. There is no one else on earth who has exactly the same gifts that you do. As you progress through this book, you will have an opportunity to gain insights about yourself that you have never discovered before. You will be guided through the easy step-by-step process of understanding how your mind is different and special. You will have a chance to try out many different psychic tools that may help you develop a special intuitive ability.

You will learn about the importance of being comfortable with your personal Belief System, the one that is truly yours, that you were born with. It can help guide you and protect you as you go through life. You will consider the possibility that you have a soul, and will come to realize that this life experience is very important to your soul's journey.

This book is designed to help each of you discover and develop your own psychic abilities, no matter how different they may be.

There is an amazing world of self-discovery and an incredible opportunity for personal and soul growth waiting for you just ahead. It is now time to give yourself permission to start your adventure with your psychic abilities.

PSYCHIC ABILITY EXPLAINED

Everyone Is Psychic

Did you know that you are psychic? You are! Actually, everyone is! But many people do not understand this special ability and it is often unwelcome and misunderstood, not only by the psychic himself, but by family, friends, and strangers alike.

Everyone was born with at least one special gift already imprinted in his/her soul. What is yours? Everything that you have experienced so far in this lifetime has helped develop your ability. Your psychic ability, like any other talent or characteristic, is a product of your physical self, your environment, your relationships, and your inherited genetics.

A PSYCHIC TRUTH

The word "psychic" comes from the Greek word *psyche*, "spirit" or "soul." In Greek mythology, the soul is personified by Psyche, a girl who loved one of the gods and suffered through many trials because of it. Through her suffering, she became a great soul (or soulful). Everyone gets his or her psychic information through an individual connection with his or her spiritual side. The way you make your connection is different from anyone else's way.

Unfortunately, the idea of being psychic often conjures up the image of gypsy fortunetellers or pay-per-minute telephone psychics. Many who claim to be psychic are really ready to fleece you out of your hard-earned money with their "mystical insights." They are masters at tricking their clients into giving them information they can use as if it came from the realm of the psychic.

Similarly, many books talk about developing and using your hidden psychic power as if it were a force that could help you control the world around you. You may be told that you can manifest your destiny, enjoy perfect health, and find wealth and prosperity with the powers you have within. As a result, many try to misuse their gifts for self-gain rather than for benefiting the Universe and helping their souls progress along the journey of understanding.

Free Will
Each soul has a map to follow during its lifetime. The map should be used as a guide to learning life lessons and resolving old karma. Whether or not you choose to follow this map is your individual choice.

Some people see life as a battlefield. They are constantly facing one crisis after another. They find themselves drained of any creative energy that could help them move forward. They do not know how to step back and find a different view of their own situation. They do not understand that their own failure to recognize their intuitive guidance system, which is in place and waiting to be set in motion, is what creates part of their dilemma.

You can't turn your psychic gift on and off like a water faucet. Once the tap is opened (whether knowingly or unknowingly), it may be difficult to shut the flow off again. Sometimes even when you want to turn it on, nothing comes through. It is a connection with the portion of yourself that flows from the soul. It is your free will to choose to become in tune with your psychic ability.

Practice Pointer

Your mind receives external stimuli through five different senses: sight, sound, touch, taste, and smell. You remember past experiences internally through these same five senses. Each of you, however, processes these memories in different ways.

The Psychic Process

Because it is different for every person, it is impossible to explain exactly what the psychic process is like. No one else has a mind that is identical to yours. Many psychic courses designed to help enhance intuitive abilities are presented in a model that the instructor uses. If you, the participant, are not of a similar mind, your initial enthusiasm can easily turn to frustration.

Remember that you are the keeper of your own ability. It is there waiting to be set into positive use. No matter what you read or others tell you, it is your soul that knows the answers. The goal is for you to be able to identify and become comfortable with your own special psychic abilities. In you, as in everyone, they are truly a gift to be shared with the world.

Your Conscious, Unconscious, and Universal Minds

There are three levels of consciousness that play a role in psychic experiences. The conscious, the unconscious, and the Universal Mind can either work with or against each other, and each person must learn to balance the messages received from these three minds.

> ## A PSYCHIC TRUTH
> When the unconscious mind takes control over the conscious mind, the individual's ability to make critical decisions is severely impaired. The result is often an action that is regretted later, when the conscious mind regains its objective perspective.

The conscious mind consists of only 10 percent of the total mind. It is in charge of reasoning, analyzing, and making critical decisions. In order for the conscious mind to be efficient, it needs to be able to maintain an objective viewpoint. This, however, is often very hard for the conscious mind to do, because it is constantly receiving input from the unconscious and the Universal Mind.

The unconscious mind is the storage facility. It retains and recalls memories that are sent up to the conscious mind at a time when it perceives that an action is needed. When this occurs, the conscious mind often accepts the suggestion and automatically sets it into motion.

The Universal Mind is the place where spontaneous insights come from. It is a direct link with the history of your soul and your guidance system, which keeps you in line with your life map or life purpose.

The Universal Mind also includes knowledge of your karma. In Buddhism and Hinduism, the word "karma" is used to relate the actions of one lifetime to each other and to make sense of how these affect subsequent lives. Unresolved karma can manifest itself through the Universal Mind, presenting an opportunity for the conscious mind to bring about resolution. You may receive intuitive warnings of possible confrontations related to karma.

Different Types of Intuition

There are three types of psychic intuition: deductive, random, and goal-focused. Deductive intuition comes from the unconscious mind; random intuition comes from the Universal Mind; and goal-focused intuition works with all three minds. Your mental makeup determines the type of intuition that is yours. Each person has a unique form of intuition that may be a blend of any of the three types.

Deductive Psychic Intuition

Deductive psychic images come from your unconscious mind's ability to take in external sensory stimuli. That's not as complicated as it sounds. Your five sensory receivers—eyes, ears, mouth, skin, and nose—are constantly bombarded with stimuli in the form of external pictures, sounds, tastes, tactile sensations, temperature changes, and smells. You take in a lot of information that you are not consciously aware of because it is absorbed by the unconscious mind, where it is stored.

When your conscious mind has a question about something that it cannot answer, this question will also go to the unconscious mind, which will mull over the problem and rely on its stored data to come up with a response. In the meantime, your conscious mind usually goes on to another subject and forgets what it was looking for. But your unconscious mind stays hard at work. All of a sudden, out of nowhere, a psychic insight appears. Your unconscious mind has come to a logical psychic solution to your problem, one that your conscious mind hadn't thought of.

Random Psychic Intuition

Random psychic intuition is different from deductive psychic intuition in several ways. It comes from your Universal Mind and may be totally unrelated to anything known or connected consciously or unconsciously to the psychic image. It could be about something that has, is, or will take place anywhere in the world. In other words, random psychic intuition can take place in any of the three phases of time—past, present, or future.

Practice Pointer

When you ask a fortuneteller to give you an answer about a specific problem in your life, the psychic will connect to her intuitive Source and focus on the requested information. Then she waits for her mind to download the information requested.

A random psychic experience often comes at a time when it is unexpected or even unwanted. It can be very powerful and leave you dazed and confused. This disorientation may last only a few moments, but its effects are powerful enough to last a lifetime. The experience itself may continue to live on in your mind long after the image first appeared.

Not all random psychic experiences are negative. It is possible that you might have a pleasant premonition; then later, you might realize that what you saw as nothing more than a happy daydream has become a reality. It may be that you suddenly get a set of numbers in your head that leads to a big sweepstake jackpot win. Or a song may begin to play in your head that you haven't heard in years, a song that later you may unexpectedly hear on the radio or television.

Random psychic intuition happens when you are in a light trance state. It occurs when your conscious or critical mind is open to the images that are sent up from your unconscious and your Universal Mind. A random psychic trance can be triggered by external or internal stimuli. Once the intuitive trance process begins, it is hard to disengage from until it has run its course.

Goal-Focused Psychic Intuition

Goal-focused psychic intuition is a combination of deductive and random intuition. Using this method, you can make a conscious effort to gain certain insights through psychic intuition. You can attempt to use your intuitive ability for a specific goal. Focused psychic intuition is the kind that is normally employed by professional psychics and others who already understand and use their intuitive abilities on a consistent basis.

Professional psychics who work with the police will often familiarize themselves with some of the facts of the case they are working on. Examining a piece of evidence or a photograph from a crime scene could provide intuitive information, and an actual visit to a specific location may also lead to new clues. Some of the information may be drawn from deductive intuition, and some may be generated at random, but all clues gathered are related to the specific goal of the psychic trance.

Traveling in and out of a Trance

When your conscious mind's ability to think clearly is interrupted, you enter the state of trance. All people, whether they know it or not, go in and out of trances many times a day. When you are in a trance, your critical reasoning becomes confused. The power of suggestion, whether it's by your unconscious mind or by someone else, takes control of your thought process.

You can be guided or induced into a trance in several different ways. The trigger can come either through external stimuli—if, for instance, you were to enter a specific location—or through internal stimuli, such as thoughts or feelings. Trances can be positive or negative, and they can continue to influence you long after your initial experience. You can remain in a trance state for a few minutes or for days. The state will continue until something interrupts it. Once you recognize the trance state, you have the choice of remaining in it or not.

Moving Through Time

Your mind moves through three different phases of time: the past, the present, and the future. Everything that you have experienced in your lifetime—your past—is deposited in the memory bank of your unconscious mind. Sometimes the information is held there for years before it suddenly comes back up to the conscious mind. When you experience these memories again, you have actually entered a memory (also called a past) trance. The stronger the memory experience, the stronger the trance.

> ### A Psychic Truth
> Sometimes a trance experience can be so powerful that the individual loses total touch with reality. This is more likely to happen when the person is in a highly suggestible state. The images that are received into the conscious mind can occur with such strength that the individual's reality shifts into the trance reality.

Your memories of the past help you construct trances relating to the future. When you experience a future event, you are entering a future trance state. The stronger you experience this image, the stronger the trance experience will be.

Your mind also experiences the present. In this time phase it can distort speed and distance. Sometimes a minute seems like an hour, and sometimes an hour seems like a minute. In athletics, being in the present is called "being in the zone."

It is easy to get caught up in such a deep trance that you are unaware of what time phase you are in. To break the trance, you must be able to balance the three phases of your mind and be aware of each one.

Psychic Trances

Psychic trances occur when your conscious mind is flooded with information that cannot be deduced by critical reasoning. Usually, this information comes from the unconscious and/or the Universal Mind. Quite often this information comes at a time when you are least expecting it. If you are not prepared, a psychic trance can catch you by surprise and may cause a great deal of mental chaos. Many people try to block this information. However, it often finds its own way to the surface again.

We all enter psychic trances. Some have a great deal of meaning, while others seem to be there just to verify that you are capable of experiencing something unexplainable. Perhaps you knew the telephone was going to ring, or you thought of a song just before it played on the radio.

Balancing Your Mind

To avoid the chaos, you need to have an inner balance of mind. Create a place in your mind where you can escape for a few moments, and learn to relax there. For some of you, this may seem like an impossibility. If relaxing for you at this time is difficult, don't worry. As you progress through the book, you will learn how to find your balance.

You may already be familiar with the term "centering yourself." Many situations in your life can keep you from being centered. You may be kept off balance by the people around you, the environment, or by psychic information when it pours through the unconscious mind. It is easy to be overwhelmed by all the stimuli, both external and internal. To help deal with life's uncertainties, you need to learn how to center yourself.

Connect with Your Third Eye

Your third eye is actually your pituitary gland. It is located in the center of your forehead, above your two other eyes. It secretes hormones that affect many of your bodily functions, including your growth and your metabolism. All three of your eyes together form the points of a triangle, a symbol that is found throughout ancient history, especially in the society of the pyramid builders. Perhaps they were aware of some lost ancient secret that helped them connect to the eye of the soul.

Practice Pointer

If for some reason you are uncomfortable about connecting to your third eye, don't feel that you have to try. All the exercises in this book are designed for you to have a positive experience. If at any time you are not comfortable, you may simply stop and return to a more positive feeling.

Focus Upward

An easy way to center yourself is to make a connection with your third eye. Those of you with a religious background may connect with your third eye when you pray. Another way to do it is through meditation. Another approach of connecting with your third eye is by doing the following exercise.

For a moment, look upward with your two physical eyes as if you were trying to see your third eye. If for some reason this is impossible or hard for you to do, that's okay; it is not actually necessary to move or see through your two eyes to experience this. You may keep your two eyes open or closed while you peek up under your eyelids. Some of you may want to squint slightly and feel your third eye. When you try this, you may feel a slight pressure in your third eye.

It may feel like it is swelling or even vibrating. You may have a feeling of warmth or coolness, or you may perceive a certain color.

Whatever you experience is okay—it's also possible that you won't feel anything at all.

Each of you will connect to your third eye in a way that is natural and correct for you. Remember, there is no one else exactly like you. No one else will have the experience that you have when you communicate through your third eye.

Now Breathe

Now let's add something else to help you center when you connect to your third eye. You may want to take a moment and find a comfortable place to sit or lie down. If any of your clothing is tight, you may want to loosen it a little. It is not absolutely necessary, but it may help you to become a little more centered. When you have done this, you may allow yourself to feel a connection with your third eye.

For a moment, allow yourself to get comfortable with the sensations you are experiencing as you make this connection. When you're ready, take a deep breath at a level that feels right for you. It may not be easy for you to inhale deeply, and that's okay. What is important is for you to breathe at a pace that helps you strengthen the connection with your third eye.

A Psychic Truth

Some people get frustrated trying to learn to meditate. They are instructed to quiet their mind, but they find it impossible to do. If your mind is that way, don't worry about it; just breathe and focus on your third eye.

Continue to breathe slowly for a few minutes. It doesn't matter whether you keep your eyes open or closed—whatever way feels right for you is correct. Your mind may just drift away. It may also be very active, with lots of thoughts suddenly popping up, or it may focus on one thing.

After you have experienced the results of this exercise for a length of time that is comfortable for you, you may take a deep breath. As you exhale, release the connection with your third eye and come back to the surface of your mind refreshed and relaxed. The more you practice this, the easier it will be to make a positive connection. Focusing on your third eye is a great way to begin connecting to your psychic mind.

Edgar Cayce, Father of the New Age

The largest impact on the advancement of psychic knowledge was made by a man named Edgar Cayce (1877–1945), who is now considered to be the founder of the New Age movement. Cayce spent much of his life trying to understand what he did while he was in a trance. While in trance, he spoke about currently unknown civilizations, in which the soul hadn't yet developed a physical body and was free to travel about without the restriction of gravity and to communicate through thought. You may have soul memories of those early times that can help in your psychic development.

An Unlikely Psychic

Cayce was an unlikely candidate for reaching the pinnacle of acclaim that he still enjoys today, over a half century since his death. He began life in rural Kentucky's tobacco country. He was close to his grandfather, Thomas Jefferson Cayce, who was said to have special psychic abilities.

Tragedy stuck one day when young Cayce witnessed the death of his grandfather in an accident with a horse. After the incident, young Edgar would visit his grandfather's spirit in one of the barns. Cayce's grandmother and mother encouraged him to continue these visits and to tell them about his experiences.

Many calamities befell young Edgar. When he was three, he fell against a fence post and punctured his skull on a nail, possibly deep enough to reach his brain. His father poured turpentine in the wound, and Cayce recovered in a short period of time. At fifteen he was hit on the spine by a ball and began to act strangely. After his father sent him to bed, he entered a hypnotic trance, telling his father what to do to cure him. Because his father followed the directions, he awoke the next morning his normal self.

When he was in his early twenties, he lost his voice. A traveling stage hypnotist temporarily helped him, and he learned to enter a self-hypnotic trance aided by a local man named Al Layne, who had taken a mail-order course on the subject. While in this altered state, Cayce was able to give himself the cure for his voice blockage. His throat turned bright red, he coughed up some blood, and his voice returned. Over the next year Cayce's voice would need further treatment on a monthly basis, and Layne, intrigued by Cayce's diagnostic abilities, experimented with his subject, hoping to uncover answers to his talent.

In 1933, Edgar Cayce and his supporters formed the Association for Research and Enlightenment for the purpose of studying, researching, and disseminating information about extrasensory perception, or ESP, as well as dreams, holistic health, and life after death. The center was located in Virginia Beach, where it still remains today.

A Psychic Truth

In 1901 Edgar Cayce began to give readings for clients. Over the next four decades he produced a body of work that consisted of over twelve thousand readings that were carefully transcribed and are still being studied today. These readings were on health, past lives, ancient mysteries such as the lost continent of Atlantis, and predictions for the future.

Cayce was able to use his psychic abilities in four different areas: precognition, retrocognition, clairvoyance, and telepathy. He had the ability to see into the future and give predictions of events to come. He could look into a person's past to find the origins of an existing health condition. He had the physical ability to see through objects and could see the inside of the human body. He was also able to enter another mind and know what the person was thinking. He could sleep on a book and remember its contents when he awoke.

Do You Recall?

Can you remember your first psychic experience? Some of you can probably recall it clearly, while others may have little or no recognition of any psychic experience at all. Chances are that it came at a very early age. You may be able to find an older family member or acquaintance who can remember that you talked about some incident that you have consciously forgotten. It could have been a series of circumstances or a single event.

All of those past experiences are stored in your unconscious mind. Even as you read these words, you may call to mind something that you haven't thought about in years. Some of you may have powerful memories connected to "unexplainable experiences" in your past. As you progress through these pages, the goal is for you to be able to define and reconnect with your special psychic gifts.

Here are a few tips for trying to remember your early psychic experiences:

* Allow yourself to be open to recalling psychic memory flashes, and don't overanalyze them.
* Don't expect to get all of the memory at once.
* Keep notes of your psychic memory flashes so that you can refer back to them.
* Once you have an idea of a possible psychic flash, talk to others who might have been aware of it at the time it happened.
* Use basic relaxation techniques to help you focus on your early psychic memory.

Practice Pointer

Whenever you are connecting to your third eye, give yourself the suggestion that you may always end your connection by opening your eyes, taking a deep breath, and connecting to your conscious mind.

Count Down

As you count yourself down, you may feel yourself sinking deeper and deeper, feeling more and more relaxed with each count. It is a very pleasant feeling, and you look forward to the next number as you count yourself downward. As you focus on your third eye, you may allow yourself to relax more and more as you open up your psychic memories. You may allow any muscles that you feel are stiff to relax. If you are ready, take a deep breath, exhale, and start counting:

5. Breathe in and out, and feel yourself relaxing more and more with each breath. Let yourself relax your muscles. As you mention the next number to yourself, you may feel yourself connecting more and more strongly with your third eye. You may feel yourself going deeper and deeper into your unconscious mind, opening up to your early psychic memories.

4. Feel yourself going deeper and deeper as you feel the connection to your third eye becoming stronger and stronger. You may breathe in and out, slowly, relaxing more and more with each breath. You may feel yourself getting closer and closer to your memories of your early psychic experiences.

3. As you breathe slowly, you may feel yourself relaxing more and more. You may feel yourself going deeper and deeper into your unconscious mind. As you get closer and closer to zero, you will be more and more connected with your unconscious mind. You will be ready to come in contact with your early childhood psychic memories.

2. You are getting closer and closer, as you sink deeper and deeper. You are relaxing more and more, and your psychic memories will be ready for you to access when you get to zero. As you breathe in and out slowly, you will allow yourself to relax more and more. You can feel your connection to your third eye more and more.

I. You are almost there. You may feel very comfortable, relaxed, and safe. You know you may always come back to a conscious state any time you want by opening your eyes, taking a deep breath, exhaling, and feeling relaxed and positive. You may allow yourself to go deeper and deeper as you count slowly backward from five to zero, each number ten times stronger than the last.

0. You may feel the connection to your third eye even more strongly than before as you are now ready to access the unconscious memories of your early childhood experiences. Anything you see, feel, hear, taste, or smell will help you to remember your early childhood psychic experiences.

Practice Pointer
While you are in a relaxed and comfortable state, you may let your unconscious memory recall images from the past that are about your early psychic experiences at a pace that is good and comfortable for you. Be aware that you can open your eyes and come back to full consciousness any time you want, feeling relaxed, calm, and refreshed.

Count Back Up
When you are ready, you may count slowly back up to your conscious mind. When you reach five, you will remember any images you may have recalled relating to early psychic experiences.

1. You are coming up and slowly releasing your connection to the third eye as you count toward five.

2. Breathe slowly and comfortably, as you count yourself back up.

3. You are getting closer and closer to the surface of your conscious mind.

4. Slowly release your connection to the third eye.

5. Now you may come fully back to the surface of your conscious mind as you release your connection to the third eye. Take a deep breath, open your eyes, and exhale. You may feel relaxed and positive about your connection to any early childhood psychic memories that you may have recalled.

Each time you perform this exercise, you may have different results. Don't expect a specific outcome. Each time you try, you may find more and different memories coming up to the surface of your conscious mind. Once you open the communication channel and continue to connect to it, the flow will become easier to access.

Near-Death Experiences and Lessons

Have you ever had a near-death experience? Was there ever a close call, during which you were inches or moments away from potential death? Did you survive a bad fall or a blow to the head? Did you have other traumatic experiences when you were young in which your mind was an important key to your survival?

Near-death experiences come in many different ways, but going through such an experience may have "jump-started" your third eye into being more open to psychic intuition.

When you go through a traumatic experience, all of your senses experience a surge in the intensity of the power of their perception. In some cases, your view of the world changes dramatically. You know something's different, but you're not sure what it is.

Children and Near-Death Experiences

A near-death experience in early childhood may often go unnoticed. Kids get into all kinds of trouble. They fall from trees, get trapped underwater, trip down the stairs, survive a car accident, or tumble off the playground swings. In some cases, such a close call may grow out of an unconscious need to escape a traumatic situation such as abuse or an emotionally unstable family.

A PSYCHIC TRUTH

Edgar Cayce had several early-life experiences that could have contributed to his psychic development. His skull was pierced with a nail at age three; he watched his grandfather die from a horseback accident; and at age fifteen he was hit in the spine with a ball. This later experience seemed to help connect him to his psychic healing knowledge.

Can you think of events in your life that may have affected your psychic ability? You are the sum total of your life to this very moment. Each new, passing moment will bring about change. As you learn to become in tune with your life, you will be more aware of your psychic abilities.

As a Child . . .

The dreams you had in your childhood could very well have been psychic in nature. Dreams, like other psychic experiences, may deal with past events or future events, or they may provide insight into situations that are occurring at the time of the dream. Dreams are a great way to receive psychic information because the conscious analytical mind is at rest, and you are open to communication from your unconscious and your Universal Mind.

Think about the dreams you had as a child. Do you remember any? If so, can you recall if they had a theme? Did you have a certain dream that occurred over and over? Can you identify the historical time period and/or location of any dreams?

Did you have symbolic dreams that may not have made sense when you had them, but that you might better understand at this point in your life? Did you have any dreams that identified situations in your life before you experienced them? Did you have recurring nightmares? Did you have dreams that were different but followed a related theme?

Did you have dreams in which dead relatives or others who had passed over communicated with you? Did you have angels, guides, or other beings or animals come to you in your sleep to comfort you and/or offer you advice? Did you ever have dreams of flying or going to places that you had never been before? Do you recall any other types of dreams that may have been of a psychic nature when you were a child?

A Psychic Truth

Here is an example of a second-sight experience. Mary remembers that as a girl, she played in the woods with other children. They taught her how to play their games. It was only later that she learned their games and clothing were from the Revolutionary War period.

You can investigate the answers to these questions in a relaxed state, as you contact your third eye. Trust your intuitive mind to give you the right answers. If you cannot remember anything, it's possible that you did not use dreams as a part of your early psychic development.

Second Sight

When you were a child, did you ever see things that were invisible to others? Did you have "imaginary friends" to play with? Could you find your way to or around a place where you had never been before?

What other experiences that might not be explainable to others did you have as a child? Did you ever have a visit from fairies or guides? Do you recall any contacts that could be considered otherworldly, such as with beings from another planet?

Déjà Vu and Learning from Past Lives

Did you ever, as a child, go to a strange place and know you had been there before? Did you experience something and feel that it had already happened? Childhood déjà vu is a phenomenon that can happen naturally. As a child, your view of reality is different because your early psychic experiences aren't limited by the boundaries that society has set for adults.

Sometimes déjà vu is so strong that second sight engages, and the experience becomes so real that the person having the experience loses touch with reality. This happens to a child more easily than to an adult, but such experiences often stay with a child into adulthood.

Past Lives

During childhood, we may still have memories from our past lives; these memories are gradually forgotten as we grow older. Do you recall any early childhood memories that can give you clues about your past lives? Did you know things about family members from different lifetimes? Did you ever act as if your role in the family were different than it should have been? Did you ever tell your family stories about other lifetimes?

Chances are, some of your psychic intuitions have come from what you've retained from your past. The more of these soul memories you can recall, the more you will find a connection to your psychic gifts.

Guidance from Within

Your inner guidance system is your connection to the Universal Mind as well as the sum total of all the wisdom and experiences you've accumulated up to this point in time. Remember that your inner wisdom and experiences come from your soul and that they transcend this one lifetime. The purpose of your inner guidance system is to help you stay on course with your life map.

Think of your guidance system as your conscience. It lets you know when something you may have said or done or left undone is inappropriate. Of course, you have the power to override your inner guidance system, and chances are you do it all the time. Everyone does. Have you ever caught yourself saying, "Why didn't I listen to myself?" It is only natural to get caught in the battle between your ego and your conscience. One is authoritative and looking for instant satisfaction, while the other wants to do the right thing.

Building Trust and Confidence

It takes time to build trust and confidence in your inner guidance system. It is the same as developing any other skill. It takes patience and the willingness to risk making mistakes as you work toward your goals. Many people are overwhelmed easily and give up because the end goal seems unobtainable.

The key to developing your trust and confidence is to start with one step at a time. If you only focus on an obstacle that is too big to climb, you will never have the opportunity to get to the top. If you work toward a small and easily achievable goal, when you reach it, you will have accomplished your short-range objective. You will then have more confidence that you can make it to your next goal. And before you know it, you have accomplished your long-term goal.

These small reachable goals are usually in tune with your inner guidance system. Each step of the way provides a balance. Giving yourself permission to take a small risk, and knowing that you have a safety net created by past success, you will become better and better at reaching toward the unknown. There is a great thrill of adventure when you are traveling in sync with your life map, in tune with your inner guidance system.

> ## A Psychic Truth
> Your own answer may come from within yourself in the form of a dream, or it may just "pop out" of your unconscious mind. It could come when you are offering advice to others, and yet the message may be for yourself. It could appear as a recurring thought that you just can't get out of your mind until you address it.

Tune In and Develop Your Gift

To tune in to your inner guidance system, you need to practice. The more you focus on developing your intuitive gifts, the more they will respond to you. If you can find a regular time once a day when you can focus on communicating with your unconscious and your Universal Mind, you will develop a habit of connecting to your inner guidance system. You will add a posthypnotic suggestion to help you with this automatic process.

If you would like to try this exercise, find a comfortable place, either sitting or lying down, loosen your clothes, take a deep breath of air, and slowly exhale. You may now focus on your third eye. As you slowly breathe in and out, you may be aware that you have many muscles; some of them are tight, and some of them are relaxed.

The more you allow the tight muscles to relax, the more relaxed you will become. In a few moments you may count down from five to zero, feeling yourself going deeper and deeper with each number. As you go deeper and deeper, you will feel your connection to your third eye becoming stronger and stronger.

Feel the Connection

As you feel the connection getting stronger, you will be aware that you are receiving a beam of light and energy that is flowing into your third eye from the Universe. This beam is good and positive, and it flows freely into your inner guidance system, carrying the wisdom of your soul.

If you are ready, you may start with the first number:

5. You are going deeper and deeper into the Universal Flow. Breathe slowly in and out as you feel the connection through your third eye getting stronger and stronger.

4. You are feeling the Universal Flow as it is received by your inner guidance system. You feel more and more relaxed with each count.

3. You may feel the vibrations of the Universe. As you go to the next number, you are more and more in tune with the flow.

2. You are getting closer and closer. Your breathing relaxes more and more. You are going deeper and deeper.

1. You are almost at the point of a deep and powerful connection to the Universal Mind. You look forward to the

last number as you take another breath and go deeper and deeper.

0. You are one with your Universal Mind and your inner guidance system.

Once the connection is complete, take a few moments to enjoy the strength and peace of the Universe. You may think of many thoughts or concentrate on just one. If you need help or guidance or have a worry, ask the Universal Mind to provide assistance and affirmation that you are in tune with your life map.

Synchronize Internal and External Messages

In addition to your channel of internal communication, you have an external guidance system of old souls who have completed their life journeys and wait to assist you. As Edgar Cayce said, the external guidance system is an "invisible empire" that exists around you.

Your external guidance system comes from the outside. It is a form of external communication from another person or entity. For instance, you may see auras or energies around others that allow you to receive helpful information. Or you may get a warning from a particular person or even from a geographic location.

Remember, these communications from the Universe can materialize at any time in almost any form imaginable, from a cloud in the sky to an encounter with an animal. All you need to do is pay attention.

Experiences of Synchronicity

One kind of external guidance experience is synchronicity. Have you ever found yourself in the right place at the right time? For some reason, exactly when you most need it, the phone rings with an answer to a dilemma. Perhaps it's an unexpected amount of money that you receive just in time to hold off a financial disaster. It could come in the mail, from a lottery ticket, from a long-forgotten debt someone owes you, or as a gift.

It is very easy to overlook synchronicity. It happens so naturally that it may not even be noticed. It's like watching a magician intently so that you may learn the trick. The magic happens right under your nose while you are focused on something else.

You're Not Alone

Are forces like synchronicity and the other external forms that your messages take all just coincidence, luck, or fate? Or is there something else involved? Perhaps you already know that someone is watching out for you. Or maybe you don't believe that there is anything at all.

Do you think that there is a being or a force that the Universe centers upon? Is there a divine purpose or a higher ideal for mankind to get in touch with? Is there a general plan for the cosmos?

A PSYCHIC TRUTH

It's all right to believe your own way. After all, that belief is already inside you. It is okay for you to compare anything you read in this book to your own feelings. The important thing is that it feels right for you.

If you have something or someone looking out for you, do you know who or what it is? You may know exactly, or you may have no idea. Just the possibility that there is something creates the opportunity for hope. You may be comfortable in a specific religion and have conversations with the Divinity to whom you turn for guidance. You may go to the seashore or the mountains and communicate with nature.

Other people believe in guardian angels who are said to watch over us. You may connect these angels to someone in your family or a friend who has passed on to the Other Side. They may come to you in your dreams, or you may feel their presence, especially in times of need.

Whatever you believe in, the purpose of this book is to give you an opportunity to explore your belief and develop your ability to connect to it.

LET YOUR BELIEF GROUND YOU

Gather Yourself and Let Go of Your Fears

Opening up to your psychic ability can be overwhelming if you are not prepared. This problem is especially evident in children and teenagers. Their first encounters usually happen without warning, and they are left confused and afraid of the unknown. Many spend the rest of their lives trying to run away from their natural gifts.

Let's consider an example. When Josh was young, he was given the opportunity to try dowsing with a forked stick. The pull of the stick was so strong that it scared him. He dropped it, and ran away. When he finally tried again as an adult, he had lost his ability to dowse. Many others have had similar experiences with different kinds of psychic talents. Perhaps you are one of them.

Practice Pointer

It is very easy when you first start developing your psychic gifts to become overwhelmed with what you encounter. If that happens, you need to stop, take a deep breath, and go back to a non-psychic activity.

Internal Self-Doubt

Opening yourself up to self-doubt can lead to confusion. The doubt begins when you do not have a clear belief that your psychic abilities have been given to you for the good of the Universe. You can create the doubt in yourself, or others can create the doubt in you.

Often, self-doubt is the result of fear. It is in your human nature to try to avoid the unknown, which by nature includes some potentially dangerous situations. But when you run from fear, it follows you and grows in proportion to your retreat. Most often you are afraid without knowing what you are afraid of. It is this fear of the unknown that can paralyze your psychic development.

When you are hit by a fear that comes from psychic intuition, you may feel very alone because you are highly aware of your difference from others and cannot confide in anyone. Many suffer in silence for years, and sometimes they take their secret fear of the unknown to their graves. As you continue through this book, you will have the opportunity to understand and resolve any fear of the psychic that you may have.

The Influence of Others

Equally damaging is advice from well-meaning people who are consumed by their own fears. If you confide in them, these people may tell you that your psychic gifts are weird or even evil. They are quick to advise you about something they do not understand. The fears of others are just as toxic to you as your own—they will contribute to your own fears and may smother your psychic gifts.

As you learn how to ground yourself and find your balance, you will be able to react to fear in a different way. You will learn to move aside and get out of the line of fire of other people's fears. You can find security in your psychic intuition and learn to trust your personal guidance system. You can replace doubt with trust.

Big Picture, Little Picture

There are two ways to focus the mind: the big picture and the little picture. As with a hologram, if you focus on only one, you may fail to see the other. As you have already read, when you focus on fear and self-doubt, you may fail to see love and the strength of the Universe. When you fail to separate your role from that of the whole Universe, you can lose focus of your own life map.

If you can only see the big picture, you are detaching yourself from your inner guidance system. You may be keeping yourself at such a distance that you are unable to take an active role in the work of the Universe. It is possible that you will not take the risk of self-improvement even though you know that is what you need to do. This inaction may cause you to feel paralyzed and unable to get on track with your life map.

When you only see the little picture, you become responsible for all of the Universe's work. You keep repeating karmic patterns over and over again and fail to see how you have an opportunity to learn, grow, and change. You are weighed down with the responsibility of not only solving your own problems, but everyone else's too. If you are like this, then you already know that others will constantly bombard you with their problems. They leave feeling better while you are left cleaning up their mess.

Role of Religion in the Supernatural

Do you rely on angels, saints, or other beings to work their good? Do you look to something to protect you from both the known and the unknown? Can you turn there when you are faced with an unknown fear?

Do you communicate with your Belief on a daily basis, just when you remember to, or only at times when you are asking for something? Do you feel that you and this higher power are compatible and in tune with each other, or do you feel as if you are in conflict?

Practice Pointer

An anchor is a neurolinguistic program (NLP) word for the process of recalling and experiencing a suggestion given while in a relaxed trance state. A touch or key word is introduced and practiced so that when it is used after the trance state has ended, the same result will be experienced again. NLP is a hypnotic technique that can bring about positive changes by installing new positive mental images in the unconscious mind.

Anchor Your Connection

You can give yourself a mental or physical anchor while you are relaxed and connected to your Belief. Put your thumb and finger together and squeeze lightly. As you do this, you may suggest to yourself that whenever you repeat this action, you will feel connected to your Belief. The level of connection will always be at the focus level that is positive and aware. In other words, if you are driving a car, you will always be alert and awake when you trigger your anchor.

The same effect can be obtained if you use a verbal anchor. A verbal anchor may be a specific word as simple as "Believe." Other types of anchors may be auditory (a specific sound), olfactory (a certain smell), or mental (the memory of a particular smell). It could even be the positive feeling you get when you are in a special place.

An anchor is a way to instantly experience a positive connection to your Belief. The more you practice making this connection, the easier it will be for you to make. If you consciously practice triggering your anchors, you will begin to do it automatically within a short period of time. The more comfortable you become communicating with your Belief, the more confidence you will have in it. It is part of the key to your psychic development.

A Psychic Truth

One concept of NLP is that the brain is like a computer—it operates on the program that has been installed in it unless a different program is installed. A "reframe" is the installation of a new mental program. This is accomplished when the unconscious mind is open to the new suggestion.

It is possible that you may already be using negative anchors, probably without any conscious awareness on your part at all. They can trigger your self-doubt. When you are connected to your psychic ability, a negative anchor may trigger and bring back an old fear or doubt. If this is the case for you, then you may use your positive belief anchor to reframe a negative one.

Put Your Belief to Work

Once you have become comfortable communicating with your Belief, you are ready to begin working with it. To begin, this means establishing a communication connection that can either remain open or be opened instantly, whenever you wish, by triggering your belief anchor(s). Your Belief is part of your inner guidance system, and when you are open to its communication, you are also working with your psychic abilities.

As you develop a partnership with your Belief, you will also become more in tune with your life purpose. This partnership is necessary for your life work—what you do during your lifetime that provides an opportunity for mankind to benefit in ways that help you and others progress in their life maps.

A great way to connect with your Belief instantly is to go through your third eye. Just feel the vibration in the middle of your forehead and believe. Take a deep breath, and exhale to add to a relaxed positive state. It is something you can do anytime. No one around you will be aware of it, except perhaps another psychic who may be observing your aura.

The Golden Light of the Universe

You can do the following exercise to receive the golden light protection from the Universal Mind, which can help you find your balance. This light comes through your Belief. It can help you dissociate and step back to get the whole view of any situation that you find yourself in or need to address. If you are ready to try it, find a comfortable place, take a deep breath, exhale, and allow yourself to relax. You may first try this exercise by counting down. However, as you learn how to develop an anchor, you can connect with your golden light anytime you want.

Practice Pointer

The golden light protection exercise is designed to help you develop a safe and secure feeling in your Belief. You are free to incorporate any image that helps you reach that state.

Count Down and Spread the Light

As you breathe slowly in and out, you may be aware that you have many muscles throughout your body. Some are tight and some are loose. Each time you feel a muscle stiffen, you may relax it, and as you are doing so, you may relax more and more. You may be aware of different muscles stiffening and relaxing as you experience this golden light exercise.

As you count yourself down, feel the beautiful golden light surround you and spread throughout your body:

5.   You may feel and see in your mind's eye a beautiful golden light that starts to flow through your third eye and down over your forehead, your face, and the back of your head. It flows all the way down to your neck. It is a wonderful,

secure, and loving light filled with all the positive vibrations of the Universe.

4. You may now feel this golden light spreading over your shoulders, down your arms to your elbows, and down your forearms, wrists, and through to your fingertips. It is a wonderfully relaxing, safe, and secure feeling. You feel the energy of the Universe flowing through and over and around your head, shoulders, arms, and fingers. As you slowly breathe in and out and feel the Universal Flow, you will go deeper and deeper into a safe, secure, and relaxed state.

3. You may feel your golden light spreading slowly down over your chest to your waist. You may feel it as it flows over the upper half of your body, wrapping you in a beautiful secure blanket of golden light. As you breathe slowly in and out, you will become more and more comfortable with this loving flow of the Universe. You are going deeper and deeper.

2. You may feel the golden light spreading down to your knees. You are in a beautiful and secure capsule of Universal Love and positive energy. As you breathe slowly in and out, you will relax more and more, and go deeper and deeper into your connection with the Universal Mind.

1. You will feel the golden light flow all the way down from your third eye to your ankles. You are almost totally immersed in the love and positive energy of the Universe. You feel comfortable, safe, and secure as you go deeper and deeper, marveling at the beauty and love of your golden universal light.

0. You are now totally immersed in your beautiful and secure golden light sent to you from the Universal Mind. You may feel this flow going through your whole body and surrounding you as a golden blanket of yellow light. Take a few moments and enjoy this beautiful, loving energy.

Filled with Your Golden Light

While you're immersed in the golden light, it is very natural to feel as if you can float up into the Universe. In fact you may begin to experience yourself lifting out of your body. If you're not prepared, it can really unsettle you. Similar experiences have turned away many first-time psychic floaters. As you have learned earlier in the chapter, the unknown can be terrifying.

As you feel yourself filling with your golden light, also see and feel a golden thread that extends down from the Universe and that is firmly anchored to the earth through you. This thread is strong enough to tether you to the ground. You may feel secure and safe if you begin to float up into the Universe because you will know that you can always follow the golden thread back to your place on earth.

Practice Pointer

This is a good exercise for you to practice. Take it slow, venturing only a small distance at first until you feel safe and secure with your golden thread tether. Each time you try, you may become more confident and comfortable with your direct connection to the Universal Mind, the keeper of your soul's memories and the holder of the knowledge of your psychic gifts.

As you progress in your psychic development, you may want to review this chapter from time to time so that you may remind yourself of your Belief and the safety of the Golden Light of the Universe. Your life may be full of little bumps and turns. Staying grounded will help you navigate along your life map.

Interact with the World Around You, Your Five Senses

You have five different ways of experiencing what takes place around you. You see, you hear, you feel (both by touch and emotion), you taste, and you smell. Some of you may be lacking in one or more of these sense receivers. It is possible that you might be blind, deaf, or have no sense of smell or taste.

A PSYCHIC TRUTH

Just as your physical genetic makeup is different from anyone else's in the world, so is your mental makeup. Understanding your mental makeup will help you communicate better, not only with yourself, but also with others. You will be able to explain your own mind and understand how someone else's mental makeup works. This will help you get your message across more easily and more effectively.

When one of these senses is lacking, another one takes over. A blind man usually has a strong ability to hear and feel. Someone who lacks the sense of taste will rely on food textures for enjoyment. Sometimes a sense is overdeveloped, and it is hard to filter out the stimulation received through that sense. The over-stimulation of one sense can cause you to go out of focus and to become unbalanced and ungrounded.

As you consider how you process information through your senses, you will find that you rely on some input more than on other. You may be very strong in one sensory arena and perhaps weak or have no input at all in another. The object is to identify how your mind works, not how to modify it to fit a certain format. Remember, there is no one else like you on this earth. You are unique and special—and your psychic ability is too.

Which Sense Is Your Strength

To help you figure out what senses you most rely on, you may try the following sense-imagery exercises. These exercises do not require privacy. In fact, you can try them with a friend or a small group. After you are done, you can compare the differences in your responses among yourselves.

Your Sense of Vision

Vision is the most commonly used sense for communication because most people are highly visual. Would you like to find out if you are, too? When you are ready, find a comfortable place, take a deep breath, exhale, and focus on your third eye. Then, consider the following questions.

Can you imagine picture images in your mind? If so, are they in color, black-and-white, or somewhere in between? Are they clear, bright, and in focus, or are they unclear and out of focus? Can you change the picture, such as seeing it in a different time, either in the past or in the future? Do you see it as a movie or as a still photograph?

Can you rewind a moving picture in your mind and watch it again, or stop it and focus on a single frame? Can you move the picture, bring it closer, push it farther away, or change the angle? Can you view it from above or from a lower position?

Can you see yourself in the picture? Can you see the picture without seeing yourself? Can you see yourself at a different age, either younger or older? Can you see colors around people in your imagination? Can you see energy forms or other elements in your mind?

Your Sense of Hearing

Next, you can examine your sense of hearing. Can you imagine sounds in your head? If so, what are they? Can you imagine music or sounds of nature, such as birds singing or the sounds of the ocean? Can you turn the volume up or down in your mind?

Can you hear conversations taking place in your head? Can you hear your own voice? Do these voices talk to you, and are they part of something other than yourself? Can you have a discussion with a voice in your head?

A Psychic Truth

If you have voices in your mind that are persistently negative and create bad thoughts for you, you should seek out a licensed mental health professional in your area for proper guidance.

Can you see a picture in your mind and hear the sounds that go with it? Can you put yourself in the picture image and move around and hear sounds or conversations from different locations? Can you watch the image as if it were a movie or a video and still be able to hear the sound? Do you picture guides or other beings who talk to you?

What You Feel

It is also important to examine your feelings. Can you imagine emotions? Are you able to experience feelings such as happiness, loneliness, or sadness in your mind? Can you intensify and weaken these emotions at will? Can you imagine visual pictures that create emotional feelings in yourself? Can you disconnect your emotions from the images in your mind? Can you step in and out of the scene, feeling and then not feeling the emotions connected to it, as you wish?

Can you feel the emotions of different people in a visual image? Is it easy to be overcome by emotional images in your mind? Do you connect emotions to certain sounds or music? Do you feel emotions in certain places or objects? Can you connect seeing, hearing, and emotional feelings in the same image?

Can you imagine feeling positive, negative, or healing energy in your mind's images? Can you imagine positive energies going through your body? Can you feel energy in terms of certain colors? Can you put yourself inside one of your mental images and imagine feeling temperatures, textures, and the weight of different objects? Could you feel the length of hair or the texture of the clothes being worn?

Your Senses of Smell and Taste

Can you imagine smells in your mind? Can you add smells to a mind's image? Can you put yourself in that picture and move around, and experience different smells? Can you intensify or weaken smells in your mind?

Can you connect smells with emotional feelings, or with sounds, foods, nature, or other mind images? Can you connect smells and tastes? Can you picture foods and connect tastes with them? Can you imagine eating a meal and tasting the different ingredients? Can you feel different emotions connected to different tastes?

PRACTICE POINTER

Now it's time to put all your senses together. Can you step into an image in your mind, and see, hear, feel, taste, and smell? Can you move about experiencing a wide variety of sensory images? Can you intensify or decrease all of your imagery? Can you step in and out of all of your sensory images?

Exercise to Open the Channel

Now that you have explored how your imagery recall works and what senses work best for you, it may be time to learn how to use some relaxation exercises to go into a self-hypnotic trance. This self-hypnosis exercise is designed for you to count yourself downward and deep inside yourself, to a place where you feel the Universal Energy that flows through your connection to the Universal Mind. It is in that place, deep inside you, that you are connected with the Universe; through that place, you become the open channel.

This exercise is designed to help you use your sense imagery to build an even stronger link through your third eye to your unconscious and your Universal Mind. By anticipating and recalling a positive memory experience, you put yourself in your "comfort zone." This process also helps sharpen your focus on something that is positive and relaxing.

Focusing on a Place

To begin, you may loosen your clothing and find a comfortable place to sit or lie down. Now, think of your favorite relaxing place. You may have a special place that you like to go to in your unconscious mind. This may be an actual place from earlier in your life, or it may be a place you currently enjoy. It could be an image of an activity or a sport that you enjoy experiencing or watching. It could be reading or watching television. Anything that you can feel that is positive can help deepen your focus.

Focusing on Your Senses

As you focus on your breathing, imagine that you are inhaling your favorite relaxing smell. If you want, you can use a smell such as incense or a candle to help you focus on your breathing. You may remind yourself that each time you smell this relaxing aroma, you will enjoy it more and more.

A PSYCHIC TRUTH

If you practice a simple exercise like this every day, you may be amazed at how it can help you relax and stay in balance. It is also helpful in conditioning your mind to go into deeper trance states that are comfortable and positive.

If you have a favorite relaxing color, you may add that to your breathing by feeling the peaceful energy every time you inhale and exhale. You may also imagine your favorite relaxing music or sounds as you breathe in and out. You may feel positive waves of energy flowing throughout your body with each slow comfortable breath you take. You may feel your muscles relaxing as these waves flow through and over you.

You may picture your image in color as full and beautiful as you can imagine. You may watch your image, or you may step into it, experiencing all its relaxing feelings. You may move around in your image and experience many different things. You may sit back and enjoy yourself as if you were being entertained at a play or movie. Just enjoy yourself for a few moments, and when you're ready, take a deep breath and open your eyes, feeling relaxed and positive.

Use Your Universal Mind

Now that you are able to go into a trance, you can use it to help you develop your psychic abilities. As you put yourself into a trance, you can combine your sensory image strengths that are part of your natural mental makeup with your third eye and your Belief and guidance systems. As you perform this exercise, remember that your way of making this connection is unique, and the script that you build for yourself is unique as well.

Creating a Script

A script is an induction read by a hypnotist to his subject to induce a trance state. It contains key words and a progressive, ever-deepening language pattern. As you are your own hypnotist, you have control of your own script.

You can write out your script if you want and make changes to it as you repeat the exercise. You can tape it, or you might choose to have someone read it to you. At first you may want to work on only one portion at a time, at least until you get comfortable with each section. You can always use aids, such as recorded music or other sounds, that help induce a trance for you. The more you practice, the easier it will be to enter a deeper state of relaxation.

Prepare Yourself

This exercise will require between ten and twenty minutes of your time. If you can plan a time when you are likely to have the fewest interruptions, the calm will help you develop your focus. If there are others who might try to interrupt, you might consider asking them to help by not bothering you for a few minutes.

Start the exercise by choosing a place where you can relax. Begin to get comfortable. Take a deep breath of your favorite relaxing smell and slowly exhale. As you continue to breathe in and out slowly, let your eyes and mind focus upward to your third eye. When you're ready, let your eyes close, and let yourself feel your connection to your third eye becoming stronger and stronger. Feel yourself drifting farther and farther away from your surroundings while still knowing where you are.

Spend a few moments just enjoying where you are. As you relax, you may anticipate yourself going deeper in a few moments.

You may let your muscles relax as you breathe in and out. You may imagine your favorite sounds and smells and let them deepen your relaxation even more. Any conscious thoughts you have may come and go as you allow yourself to relax.

Practice Pointer

If for some reason an exercise makes you uncomfortable, just open your eyes and think of something positive. Then you can feel free to resume your daily activity. You may also remind yourself that you will go to a trance depth that is appropriate for the moment and that, in trance, you will be aware of your surroundings.

Counting Down

You may now feel your third-eye connection—the Golden Light of the Universe—as it prepares to spread throughout your body. You may feel very positive and relaxed as you enjoy its protective energy. If you are ready, you may begin counting downward from five to zero as you prepare to experience a pleasant memory image in all your five senses. It may be the same image every time or a different one, real or imaginary:

5. Take a deep breath and feel the golden light from the Universe begin to spread down through your third eye over your forehead, eyes, nose, cheeks, back of your head, mouth, chin, and neck, to your shoulders. You may feel yourself sinking deeper and deeper as though you were descending a stairway to the very center of your

unconscious and through to your Universal Mind. With each step, you will go deeper and deeper as your connection gets stronger and stronger.

4. You may now feel the golden light spread over your shoulders and down your upper arms, your elbows, forearms, wrists, and fingers, all the way to the fingertips. As you breathe in and out, you may feel yourself going deeper and deeper. You may relax more and more as you feel the protective energy of the Universe.

3. You may feel yourself going deeper as you feel the golden light spread down over the upper part of your body, over your chest and back, and all the way to your waist. You may also feel yourself wrapped in the protective bubble of Universal Energy. You may focus on your favorite sound or smell as you slowly breathe in and out. You feel the third eye and the connection to the Universe is even stronger and stronger as you feel the power of the positive protective energy that flows through you. You are going deeper and deeper.

2. The positive energy of the Universe is now spreading all the way down to your knees as you feel yourself going deeper and deeper. Any positive imagery you experience is getting clearer and clearer as you focus on the beauty and powerful energy of the Universal Mind. You may feel yourself sinking deeper and deeper inside as you continue going down to the place where you are in full contact

with the Universe. It is a place where you can feel safe and protected, far away from the conscious world around you.

1. You are almost at that special place. You may feel the golden light spreading down to your ankles as you go deeper and deeper. You feel your focus becoming clearer and clearer as you drift away from your conscious thoughts. The protective energy flows around and through you.

0. You are in a deep state of communication with the Universal Mind. You feel yourself totally wrapped in the protective energy of the universal golden light that is spreading throughout your entire body.

Exploring Your Senses

Let yourself focus in on your visual image. You may be able to see colors or energy. Whatever you see, remember that it is positive and compatible with the universal golden light. Put yourself in the image, and then let yourself watch from a distance. Each time you experience it, you will see something that is important to focus on. Continue to breathe in and out, feeling relaxed and connected to the protective energy of the Universe.

A Psychic Truth

This is an excellent method to help you strengthen your focus. At zero, you can practice getting clear images in each one of the five senses. Try to change your perspective as you experience your image. The more comfortable you become, the more it will help your psychic development.

Now focus on your hearing sense. Imagine sounds that are relaxing and positive. Turn the volume up or down, and slow the sounds down or speed them up. Adjust what you are hearing until the sounds are in the proper balance for you. The more you are comfortable, the more you will focus. If you can hear pleasant conversations going on within your image, let yourself listen in, and move about from different viewpoints.

Next, add in your kinesthetic sense to get the feel of the image and the moods. Experience different textures, temperatures, and emotions. Now include tastes and smells. Let yourself drift through a virtual reality of your different senses. Spend as long as you want there, feeling safe and secure as you explore the regions of your unconscious and your Universal Mind.

Anchor Your Experience

Before you leave and return to the surface of your conscious mind, give yourself word and touch anchors that will help you recreate your connection with your sense imagery. Choose a word that brings back this special feeling. Say it to yourself several times, experiencing how you feel when you are connected to your Universal Energy. Do the same thing with a touch, such as a thumb and finger pressed together.

While you are still in your deep relaxed state, suggest to yourself that each time you experience this exercise or use your anchors, you will become more and more comfortable with the way you process your five sense images. You may tell yourself that your abilities are given to you by the Universe to be used for the good of both yourself and others.

You may suggest that anytime you need it, the universal bubble of golden light is there to surround you and protect you. It is a suggestion you can use everyday. This will be helpful as you experience the various psychic development exercises in the upcoming chapters of this book.

Back to the Surface

When you are ready, you may begin to count yourself back up to the surface of your conscious mind, from one to five:

1. You are relaxed and refreshed as you begin your journey back. Breathe in and out slowly and comfortably. All your tensions have disappeared.

2. You continue upward. The positive images and Universal Energy are still vivid in your mind. The golden light escorts you as you continue your journey back to consciousness. You feel so relaxed and positive.

3. You are halfway there. You look forward to bringing your experiences back to the surface to assist you as you move about the conscious world.

4. You can see the surface of your conscious mind just ahead. As you come to the last number, take a deep comfortable, relaxing breath.

5. Exhale, open your eyes slowly, and come back to the surface of your conscious mind, relaxed, refreshed, and still filled with the Golden Light of the Universe.

Take a few moments to readjust to the world about you. Keep this positive experience with you as you go on about your day or evening.

The Seven Energy Centers in Your Body

The word "chakra" comes from the Sanskrit word for "wheel." Hindu and Buddhist religions believe that the human body has a series of energy centers. These centers act as openings for universal energies to pass through the body's aura. Like wheels, the chakras vibrate and turn at different speeds to help receive and distribute the energy.

There are seven major chakra centers in the human body, as well as many minor ones. Note that each chakra center has a related endocrine gland that secretes hormones. The better your energy centers and your glands work together, the greater the opportunity is for your body, mind, and soul to be in harmony with each other. The seven chakra centers are the following:

1. The base, or root, chakra (Muladara). The lowest of the seven major centers, this chakra is located at the base of the spine and is the simplest of the seven. It relates to your physical strength and animalistic nature, as well as the senses of taste and smell. It is in the base chakra that the kundalini energy waits in coiled readiness to respond to your basic needs. (According to the Yogis, kundalini energy is the psycho-

spiritual energy that is a powerful source of many psychic experiences.) This chakra controls the gonads.

2. The sacral, or belly, chakra (Svadishana). Located just below the navel, near the genitals, the sacral chakra controls sexual energy and reproduction and may affect your health when out of balance. It influences the release of adrenaline in your body and can keep it on a high state of alert when influenced by stress. This chakra also controls what is known as the cells of Leydig, testicular or ovarian cells that secrete testosterone.

3. The solar plexus chakra (Manipura). Located below the breastbone and above the navel, the solar plexus chakra is the center where mediums get their psychic information. The solar plexus chakra controls the adrenal glands; when it is out of balance, it can affect your stomach, liver, and pancreas.

4. The heart chakra (Anahata). Located in the center of the chest and in the middle of your shoulder blades, the heart chakra relates to the Universal Mind and emotions such as love, honesty, and caring. f it becomes blocked, it can affect your heart, lungs, and breathing. It also rules your thymus gland.

5. The throat chakra (Visudda). Located at the top of the throat, the throat chakra relates to creativity, self-expression, and

the creative arts, including music, art, and writing. When its center is blocked, your throat, ears, eyes, nose, and mouth may be affected. This chakra rules the thyroid gland.

6. The forehead, or third eye, chakra (Ajna). Located between your eyebrows in the center of your forehead, the forehead, or third eye, chakra relates to your pituitary gland and your psychic ability. When this center is blocked, it can affect your head, eyes, and brain.

7. The crown chakra (Sahasrara). Located at the top of your head, the crown chakra will not open until all six of the other chakras are balanced. When it is open, you experience the highest connection to the Universal Mind by your mental, physical, and spiritual self. The crown chakra controls the pineal gland.

The Universal Life Force enters the body through the crown chakra at the top of the head. As it works its way down through your body, it flows through the other centers. As it spreads to the base chakra, it arouses the kundalini energy, which yogis believe sleeps in a coiled serpentine form.

Balance Your Chakras

It is possible that one or more of your chakras may be blocked as a result of many different situations. The cause may be stress, or it could be a mental, spiritual, or physical condition. Be aware that it is almost impossible to keep all of your chakras in balance all the time.

Once you grow sensitive to feeling the balance of your chakras, you will be able to sense when the balance is broken. At that point, you can take the steps to bring yourself back in balance.

The goal of this basic balance exercise is to open your third-eye chakra to the Golden Light of the Universe and let it flow downward through your other centers until it reaches your base chakra. When that is achieved, let it radiate upward, opening the crown chakra. This will help you begin to balance the energy throughout your body. As you get comfortable with the circulation of the Universal Flow, it may seem as if you are literally taking in this positive energy with each deep breath.

A Psychic Truth

If the chakra is opened and not balanced, the flow of energy may be overwhelming. This is particularly true when you open yourself to psychic energy. It can pulse through you and totally immerse you without warning. Knowing how to shut down the flow is as important as knowing how to open it.

Let's Begin

You may start by getting comfortable. Take a deep breath and exhale slowly. Do this a couple more times, allowing yourself to relax more and more with each breath. If any muscle is stiff, allow it to relax as you continue to breathe slowly in and out. You may now close your eyes and focus on your third-eye chakra.

Allow yourself to feel the Universal Energy as it streams at a comfortable rate into your third eye. You may feel the warmth of love and peace from the golden light of the Universal Energy as it continues to flow downward. For a few brief moments, allow yourself to absorb this peaceful and loving feeling, as each breath brings it more and more into focus.

Feel the Universal Energy Flow Downward

You may allow yourself to focus on this loving and peaceful energy as it moves downward to your throat chakra. As the energy reaches this center, you may feel the universal vibration first relax and then open that area of your body. You may feel the love and peace that flows through the golden energy and light of the Universe from your third eye to your throat with every deep breath you take. Take a few moments to enjoy this blend of energy as it resonates with each breath, in through your third-eye chakra and out through your throat chakra.

Now allow your Universal Energy to flow downward until you focus on your heart chakra. Feel the peaceful and loving energy as it brings the warmth of the golden light and energy of the Universe to your heart. Feel the vibrations as they tune this important center around your heart. You may feel the loving and peaceful energy with each deep breath as it flows in through your third eye, down to your throat, and out through your heart chakra. Take a few moments and enjoy the love and peace as it spreads through and balances these three chakras.

A Psychic Truth

Your spine is the main conduit for the Universal Energy flow. As you breathe in, focus on the love and peace that is entering through your third eye. As you breathe out, feel the love and peace flowing through the energy center that you have focused on.

Continue to Move Down

Now you may feel the peace and love of the Universal Energy as you focus it downward to your solar plexus chakra. Feel the positive vibrations of your solar plexus center balancing itself as you breathe the Universal Energy in (through your third eye to your throat and heart chakras) and out (through your solar plexus chakra). With each deep breath you take, the golden light of the Universal Energy flows downward as you feel its peace and love. Take a few moments and enjoy the special sensations created by the balancing of these energy centers.

The Power of Kundalini Energy

Now, when you are ready, allow yourself to focus the peace and love of your Universal Energy flow down to your sacral chakra. As you feel the golden light vibrations bring balance to this center, you may be aware of the kundalini energy that waits below, coiled and ready to combine its strength and power with the Universal Flow. With each deep breath, you may feel the peace and love of the Universe as it flows down through your third-eye chakra, to your throat, heart, and solar plexus, and out through your sacral chakra. Take a few moments to enjoy the peace and love of the Universe as it flows downward through your centers.

Now you may allow yourself to focus the Universal Flow downward all the way to your root chakra. Feel the power of the kundalini energy as it combines with the Universal Energy and lifts it upward. As you breathe downward, the universal golden light flows through your third eye, to your throat, heart, solar plexus, navel, and out through your root chakra, as you feel peace and love. As you exhale, you may feel the vast power of the Universe as it pulsates throughout your entire body. As your six chakras vibrate in total harmony, they now open your crown chakra to the divine wisdom of the Universe.

Energy Flow Through Your Crown Chakra

Spend some time in this peaceful and loving state as you experience the divine energy of the golden light flowing throughout your body. Your head may naturally feel as if it is lifting upward so your third eye can have a direct connection to the Universal Energy flow. You may slowly allow your arms to open and float up from your body. Your hands may open with their palms cupping slightly and facing upward to further receive the peace and love of the Universe.

You may feel the incredible power of the Universe as it combines with your internal and external guidance systems and your Belief. At this time, you are totally open to the peace and love of the Divine. In this state, your intuitive gifts are now in balance and harmony. You are ready to receive the appropriate knowledge provided by the Universe for your psychic development.

Count Back Up

When you are ready to come back to your conscious mind, you may count slowly from zero to five. As you continue to breathe slowly and deeply, you may bring your feeling of peace and love back to your conscious state. When you get to five, take a deep breath, open your eyes, and continue to feel the positive flow of the Universe through your balanced chakra centers. You may feel grounded in the divine love of the Universe.

This exercise is very basic. If you want to incorporate your own techniques, you are encouraged to do so. Each of you will have a different experience as you work with your chakras.

Keeping Energy Centers Open with Massage and Color Therapy

If you would like to help your energy centers open, you may want to consider adding light massage techniques to your balancing exercise. As you focus on your third-eye chakra, you may gently massage the center of your forehead. Move the three longest fingertips of one of your hands in a circular motion. After a few moments, let your hand return to its previous position as you focus on the peace and love that are balancing the third-eye chakra.

When you focus on the throat chakra, continue this same massage technique. Always keep your touch light as you move your hand slowly in a circular motion. If for any reason you feel discomfort, discontinue the massage and either focus on your chakra exercise without it or open your eyes and come back to full consciousness, relaxed, calm, and filled with peace and love.

Another method of massaging your energy centers is to work with your aura. Place the open palm of one of your hands approximately two inches above an energy center. Slowly begin to circle the palm of your hand in a counterclockwise motion. You may feel pressure, heat, a tickle, or a prickly feeling as your hand moves over the spot.

Practice Pointer

When a blocked energy center is opened suddenly, the rush of energy can trigger a spontaneous psychic image. This often is the case when you experience massage, Reiki, or another method of healing art for the first time.

Restoring Balance Through Color

Each of the seven energy chakras also has a specific color that is produced when the energy of that center is in balance. If you are visual, it may help you to balance your chakras by visualizing the proper color for each center. You may add the color imagery to your chakra balancing exercise. Here is a list of colors for each of the seven chakras:

* The base, or root, chakra is red.
* The sacral, or belly, chakra is orange.
* The solar plexus chakra is yellow.
* The heart chakra is green.
* The throat chakra is blue.
* The third-eye, or forehead, chakra is a deep indigo.
* The crown chakra is a white or pure light.

You may be able to feel energy in relationship to color. You can focus on red and go right to your root chakra and feel the base of your kundalini energy. Or you can focus on the color green and project it to your heart chakra.

As you begin to practice getting in tune with your energy centers, you may want to practice opening and balancing them in a natural progression from your third eye downward and finally back to the crown. The more you understand the vibrational level of each center, the more it can help you in your psychic development.

Chakras and Your Psychic Development

You may already have had a psychic experience through one of your different chakra centers when you unwittingly opened up to the Universal Flow. When it happened, you might not have been aware of what took place. This explanation may help you get a better perspective on what may take place when you have a psychic experience through one or more of your chakras.

The lower chakras are considered to be more primitive in the range of psychic abilities. It is through the root, sacral, and solar plexus energy centers that you open to being a medium or to communicate with the dead. You may also use these chakras when you experience psychic dreams. The lower chakra levels are considered to be more spontaneous than controlled.

The heart chakra is where you intuitively feel. If you are working with massage or other healing techniques and open your heart chakra, you may be flooded with the other person's physical, mental, or spiritual negative feelings. If you aren't prepared for the energy flow, you may find yourself internalizing it. Without an outlet, this energy will overrun yours, and it may affect your balance and even your health. If, on the other hand, you have some awareness of what might happen, you can let the energy flow through your heart chakra. Channeled this way, it has a great potential for healing those who receive the positive energy of peace and love.

When your throat chakra is open, you may have the ability to hear your guides or angels. You may receive verbal advice or even warnings about yourself or others. (You will have the opportunity to experiment with clairaudience in an upcoming chapter.) As you identify and learn to rely on the communication that comes to you through your guides, you will learn to trust their accuracy.

A PSYCHIC TRUTH

The ability to see psychically is called clairvoyance. When your third-eye chakra is open, you may be able to see on nonphysical planes. You may see as well as hear your guides or angels. You may also be able to see the past or future.

When the crown chakra is open, you may be able to travel to and experience different planes. It is through this center that you may be able to visit the Akashic Records, as Edgar Cayce did over fifty years ago. You may find yourself floating out of your body and experiencing the vast power of the Universal Flow.

Practice and Document Your Experiences

Now you may go back to your chakra exercises and begin to identify your psychic gifts. First, let yourself come into balance with all your energy centers. It is always good to center yourself when starting a psychic exercise. Do this by connecting to your Belief and your internal and external guidance systems. Feel the peace and love of the Universe and believe that any intuitive image is given to you for a special purpose.

Once you have done this, start with your lower chakras and open up to connections from the Other Side. You may feel the power of the kundalini as it combines with the Universal Flow. You may open to spontaneous psychic intuition that is given you by the golden light and energy of the Universe.

When you are ready, open your heart chakra to healing energies and positive feelings. Next open your throat chakra to the communication of your guides and angels. Look for the clear visions through your third eye, and finally let yourself float to other planes of psychic experiences guided by the golden thread along the white beam of your crown chakra. When you are ready, slowly bring yourself back to consciousness, filled with the love and peace of the Universe and in tune with your psychic experience through your chakras.

Remember, the way you work through your energy centers is different from anyone else. You may experiment with all the material in this chapter and develop a technique that is best for you. As you work with your chakras, you may find yourself opening more and more to your psychic gifts.

Clairvoyance Is a Visual Gift

"Clear Seeing"

You see with your conscious mind as well as with your unconscious and your Universal Mind. Your conscious images are experienced live—what you are seeing is happening at that moment. Conscious sight is the reality, as it is shared with other people. When you experience a conscious visual image, it is then stored in your unconscious memory.

The unconscious mind is capable of replaying a stored conscious visual image at a later time. Your unconscious mind will replay the image in the way that your conscious mind processed it. Five people might all share the exact same experience and then recall it, through their unconscious minds, differently. Each one may get part of the experience correct and part of it wrong. Each person is replaying what he recalled from the experience when it actually happened.

A Psychic Truth

Clairvoyance literally means "clear seeing." A psychic who is clairvoyant has the ability to see what is generally acknowledged to be unseen or not real. A psychic who understands her power of clairvoyance accepts it as part of her reality.

Second Sight

In addition to your external visual reality experiences, you may also have the gift of clairvoyance, or second sight. Some of you may already be aware of and using this gift; others may have chosen to try to ignore or block it. Second sight may appear to you at any time, usually when you are least expecting it.

Second sight can combine with your other senses and may be experienced in all three phases of time—past, present, and future. The past images may come from your present lifetime or from a time period back in history. They may relate to your life or they may have nothing to do with it.

Second sight into the future means seeing something that has not yet happened. These images may just "pop" into your head and cannot be related to anything that is currently taking place in the reality of the moment. If your third-eye chakra is open and unbalanced, you may receive second-sight images relating to any place in the world. In other words, you may be overrun with psychic garbage.

Realistic and Symbolic Visual Images

There are two different ways that you may experience clairvoyance. The most common way is to see a realistic visual image. It can come to you either when you are awake or when you are asleep and may relate to the past or the future. It can also be triggered by what you are experiencing at a particular moment in time.

The other form of second sight is symbolic. Symbolic imagery often involves the kinesthetic sense. The images may provide you with a "gut feeling" of their meaning. All psychics must learn to develop their own interpretations of the symbols they visualize.

How Do You See?

There are several different types of clairvoyance, including the ability to see through objects, over long distances, into the past (an ability known as retro-cognition), or into the future (known as precognition). Clairvoyance may involve being able to see health conditions of people and/or animals, having psychic dreams, visualizing other worlds and beings, and seeing divine images.

A Psychic Truth

Mental telepathy is mind-to-mind communication and is part of your range of psychic abilities. Visual telepathy is the communication of a visual image from one person to another. It is different from second sight or clairvoyance because only your mind is involved.

You may be able to have psychic experiences in all of the different ways, or in some, or in none. Your mental makeup will help determine whether you have the potential to experience and develop the psychic abilities of second sight.

Many people with the gift of second sight can see into the future or the past, whether through dreaming or contact with spirits, angels, or guides. The more you become aware of and understand what you are already seeing in your mind's eye, the more confidence you will have in trusting and using your psychic gifts in the future.

Clairvoyant Visions and Connections

One aspect of clairvoyance is seeing spiritual beings like angels or spirit guides. Note that this isn't the same as seeing ghosts, who contact you on a physical plane. A spirit usually contacts you from your inner mind—either your unconscious or your Universal Mind—and its vision materializes in your mind's eye.

Spirit guides can help you navigate successfully through your life map. They have the ability to communicate with your Universal Mind and to gather wisdom that will help you make positive decisions. Although they most often appear in human form, they may be experienced in other shapes as well.

Practice Pointer

Learn from your dreams—they may be of symbolic nature, especially if they involve a specific animal or other spirits. If you can see spirits in your dreams, you have an even greater opportunity to develop an understanding of how they are here to work with you.

Visions of the Past and Future

Precognition is a more unmediated form of psychic ability. This gift is more direct because it can allow you to see an event as it will happen in the future, rather than having a spirit guide who will share information with you regarding what is going to happen. Most often, precognition works as a realistic image, but it can also be viewed in symbolic form. The event can be recognizable and related to you or someone you know, or it can be something that you know nothing about. You may see it only once, or it can occur over and over. It can come to you in a dream or a vision.

The earliest psychic images a young person may receive are often precognitions. They appear out of nowhere, and, more often than not, they predict an event that is related to an impending tragedy—the death of a loved one or an accident. Once a young person has seen signs of the future event in his mind and sees it actually happen, he may feel responsible for the event and believe that he caused it to happen.

Looking Back at the Past

The opposite of precognition is postcognition—seeing into the past to events that have already occurred. The images could be related to the individual's own lifetime or to something not closely connected to her. A location or an object may help induce a postcognition trance. The event seen could even be from a distant lifetime or time period.

One form of postcognition is time bending. There are those who believe that they can merge different time periods for the purpose of healing the past. They project themselves back into events from the past so that they may release the negative aura that may have been trapped in that time period. It is believed that if mankind can heal history by resolving the mistakes of the past, the future will not be caught in the same unresolved karma.

Embarking on an Imaginary Adventure

Have you ever experienced any of the visual images discussed so far and dismissed them as just your imagination? If so, you are not alone. Many people never give their psychic ability of second sight a chance to help guide them through life. Perhaps you have dismissed psychic images that you have experienced in the past as just "your vivid imagination." But was that really all it was?

If you have a good visual imagination, it is all right to let it take you on an imaginary adventure. You don't have to worry about what you imagine just yet—it doesn't necessarily have to be psychic information. If you spend a lot of time imagining negative possibilities, maybe that is happening because you are not spiritually grounded. When you are worried about an unknown result, ask your Belief or spiritual guide to help you. And if you begin to feel uncomfortable, you may always discontinue the session by taking a deep breath and returning to your conscious mind.

Practice Pointer

When you let your imagination flow, always make sure you are grounded. By connecting yourself to your Belief and the Golden Light of the Universe, you are taking steps to protect yourself from any negative images that you may experience.

As you let your imagination run wild, make note of your thoughts and compare them to events in the real world. These notes may record events that have already happened—that is, from the past—but you should also note events that happen in accordance with the way you envisioned them. It is okay for you not to fully understand the process that is taking place as you imagine. All you really need to understand is that imagination is an ability that you have. Just accept it and allow yourself to take a very large step in your psychic development. The more you work with it, the more you will learn to trust your psychic gift of second sight.

Exercise Your Gift

Psychic visual experiences differ from person to person. Your particular vision may come from either inside yourself or from an outside source. The goal here is to encourage you to identify, develop, and work with your visual psychic abilities. And the first step is to identify how you see.

It is very possible that you may have a gift of second sight that is different from those addressed in this chapter. Your mind is special and unique. It does have psychic abilities, but they may or may not be visual. If you do have the gift of clairvoyance, it is likely connected to one or more of your other four senses.

Second-Sight Exercises

The following exercises will help you identify and begin working with your visual psychic abilities. Although you can do these exercises on your own, it can be both fun and educational to do them in a group setting. When you compare your second sight to that of others, you may be amazed at how different or similar they are. You can always record the scripts and play them back, or have another person read them out loud. You can also experience them as you read them to yourself.

PRACTICE POINTER

When you begin to practice psychic development exercises, it is very important for you to be in tune with your physical, mental, and spiritual self. This includes being spiritually grounded, in the proper frame of mind, and having a full stomach.

What's under Your Eyelids?

You may begin this exercise by finding a place that is comfortable and relaxing for you. You can either sit or lie down. When you're ready, take a deep breath, exhale slowly, and let your eyes go out of focus as you concentrate for a moment on your third-eye chakra. You may take a few moments and experience the rest of your energy centers coming into balance. As you continue to breathe slowly in and out, you may feel the loving and peaceful energy of the Universe entering your body. You may feel a protective bubble of universal golden light surrounding you as you examine your psychic gifts of second sight.

When you are comfortable and ready, focus your mind's eye on the images that are behind your eyelids. You may see an image clearly, or it may be out of focus. It is possible that the images you see are moving so fast that it is hard to focus on any one of them. If that is the case, allow yourself to relax even more and begin to slow down the speed of your images. This may be hard to do at first, but as you continue to practice, you should be able to bring your images into sync with your focus.

If you are able to see images under your eyelids, what are they? How do they compare to the different types of second sight that were discussed earlier in this chapter? Are they similar or different? Are your images comfortable or uncomfortable? If an image is uncomfortable, can you change it to another image? Can you interpret your images to understand their meanings?

You might ask your Universal Mind to help provide you with answers to any questions you may have. The answer may not come right away. Be patient, and remain alert to your insights. The answers may come from within or without.

Can you get images about the past or the future? Can you see your guides, or angels? Do you have images that relate to health or to your Higher Power? Are there any other images that you can see under your eyelids, and can their meanings be understood? When you are ready, take a deep breath, exhale, and return to consciousness in a positive relaxed mood.

Dream Imagery

Another exercise is to explore your dreams. As you relax and concentrate on your third eye, think about the dreams you've recently had. Do you dream in pictures? If so, are your dreams symbolic, realistic, or do you experience both types? Do you travel to and explore places in your dreams? Do you dream of past lives or future events? Do you see guides, angels, or loved ones who have passed over in your dreams?

A PSYCHIC TRUTH

Another great way to work with your psychic intuition is simply to close your eyes and imagine. You might imagine a story with a theme that relates to your current life or from any point in time. Through this exercise, you may find insights that relate to your life. Imagination is often a great method for finding the truth.

See the Second Image with Your Eyes Open

Have you ever had a second-sight experience when your eyes were wide open? If so, it may seem natural to you. If you rarely do or have not had the opportunity to experience it, however, here is a suggestion for an exercise to try. Allow yourself to enter a relaxed state as you focus for a moment on your breathing.

Focus on your third-eye chakra. Your eyes will go slightly out of focus as you put yourself into a light hypnotic trance. You may suggest to yourself that you are comfortable and open to the psychic images that are waiting to help you grow in your intuitive development. Let your mind drift as you enjoy your connection to your visual energy center.

You may begin to be aware of a second image in your visual screen. Wait patiently and let this image slowly become clearer and clearer as it comes into focus. Let yourself see it clearly as you watch from the safety of your protective bubble of golden light. Allow yourself to watch and process this image, and know that you can end it anytime you want and return relaxed and positive to your conscious mind.

Keep a record of what you see and when you see it. Does your second sight relate to the past or the future? Are there times and places where it is easier to get these images? Can you look at a person and see energy or auras around her? Do the auras change?

Can you look into a person's body and see a medical problem? Can you create a healing image? Can you project your mind's eye to a remote location and see what is happening at that very time there?

Record Second-Sight Success

As you begin to develop your psychic abilities, keep a record of what you experience. Just like learning or honing any skill, the more you practice, the sharper and stronger your second sight will become.

At first, you may not receive many images—or you may get so many that they confuse you. Remember, patience is the key word. After all, what you are doing is getting back in touch with natural psychic gifts that have been with you for a very long time.

"Clear Hearing"

Clairaudience literally means "clear hearing," and in psychic terms it is the ability to hear voices, sounds, or music that doesn't exist on the "normal" plane. These sounds may be internal, or they may exist on a different plane, in a different lifetime or location. If you have the gift of clairaudience, you can hear more than most other people.

Man has been guided by his internal voice since the beginning of time. The Bible makes reference to the Voice of God speaking to the prophets. The ancient Greeks received guidance from *diamons*. The shamans of many cultures used the voices in their heads for divine advice.

A PSYCHIC TRUTH

Diamons are divine spirits that offer wisdom, usually through internal voices. Communication with a *diamon* was an accepted form of psychic guidance until the Christian church classified *diamons* as demons, servants of the devil.

A Voice in Your Head

Today clairaudience is identified in many different forms. You may hear your own voice or one or more other voices. These voices may be heard as spirit guides, angels, deceased relatives or other spirits, symbolic figures, divine wisdom, or even animal guides. These voices may come when you are awake or in your dreams.

You may only hear a voice when you have a specific need, or you may receive regular guidance from it—and there may be several different voices that you can perceive at different times. You may be able to project yourself out into the Universe and have a conference with brilliant minds on the Other Side.

You may be able to channel the voice of your spirit guide or let the voice of a departed spirit speak through you. You may hear the spirit's message and be able to repeat it word for word. You may actually become the other personality and lose your style of speaking or even your thought process. This is usually done while one of you (yourself or the medium) is in an altered state of consciousness, as during a séance.

Sounds and Music

Besides voices, certain sounds may provide you with psychic insights. Some people hear ringing in both or one of their ears as a warning from the Universe. You may already be receiving such a communication without even realizing it. If you have sounds in your head, pay attention to their possible meanings.

Do you hear music in your mind? Have you ever had a song pop into your head and a short time later heard it being played on the radio or television? If so, what does that mean? It could be your spirit guides telling you to pay attention to other messages that may give you psychic insight. There is always a meaning to the messages, sounds, or music, and sometimes when you hear them you are merely receiving a confirmation of your intuitive gifts.

External Voices, Sounds, and Music

Besides the voices, sounds, and music in your mind, you may be able to hear real voices, sounds, and music that most others cannot hear. This may be due to very sensitive hearing, much like an animal that hears an arrival long before most humans can. For example, you may hear music being performed from a different time period if you are in the place where it was played before.

You may be able to hear spirits who exist around the area where you hear them. They may try to communicate with you, or they may just go on about their business, reenacting a scene from their life as if you were not there. You may eavesdrop on a celebration, a dance, an argument, or a battle. All of these activities run their own course with or without you.

A PSYCHIC TRUTH

Some of you may be able to hear the sounds of another time period. The sound may be one that has left an impression on the location or on an object. It may also be possible for you to project yourself into the future and hear the sounds of future events.

You may externally hear the voices of your guides, angels, or those who have passed over. They may be a direct communication to and for you. It may be hard to determine if the voice, sound, or music is in your mind or if it is external and heard by your ears. It really doesn't make a difference as long as you accept it as a positive reality. The more you become aware of and trust your external voices, the more you will develop your psychic intuition.

Hearing Someone Else's Thoughts

You may be able to tune into what someone else is thinking. Let's take a look at another example. Betty has the gift—she thinks it's a curse—of hearing negative thoughts from other people. She can be in a crowded room and all of a sudden hear an angry voice in her head just as if it had been spoken out loud. She tries to tune the voices out, but if she drops her protection, they filter back into her mind. Communicating with someone else's thoughts is a form of mental telepathy that will be covered later in this book. Do you have this ability? Let's explore it.

Opening Your Throat Chakra

The energy center for clairaudience is in the throat area. When it is open, you may be able to receive communications from your psychic sources. If you inadvertently open your throat chakra when it is not in balance, you may open yourself to more than you want to hear. On the other hand, if you block your throat chakra, you may find yourself frustrated, as this blockage may result in your not being able to receive your internal guidance.

As with other types of psychic abilities, effective use of clairaudience depends on the receiver. You are the mechanism through which the voices, sounds, and music are received. If you are not in total alignment with the signal, you may miss or hear incorrectly the messages from beyond. It is important to take proper care of your gift of hearing.

Listen to Internal Noise

As with other psychic functions, you may at first question any clairaudient gifts that you may have. It is easy to excuse a psychic event as an accident in synchronicity. Rational thinkers will always have a manifest-reality reason for everything. It is hard for them to accept a reality other than the one they are used to seeing, hearing, and feeling. At the same time, there are those who look at every event as a psychic happening. Your ability to step back and see both views is very important to the success of your psychic development.

When you try the clairaudient exercises, you may hear all your different voices, sounds, and music without worrying for now about whether they are real. The goal is for you to gather the information first. Once you have done that, you can compile your experiences to see what feels right for you. It is possible that some people will not understand or believe your psychic experiences. Don't worry about it. They need to come to terms with their own psychic abilities, and it may happen sooner or later, whether in this lifetime or at a later date.

A Psychic Truth

It's okay not to be able to explain your clairaudience. You may have many clairaudient talents, or you may have one or even none. If the hearing sense is not your strength, another one will be.

Internal Clairaudience Exercise

If you would like to begin this exercise, find a comfortable place to relax, either sitting or lying down. It is good if you are in a place where you will not be interrupted for at least a half an hour. If you are worried about falling asleep, set an alarm or have someone check on you at the time you wish to end your exercise. You may have someone read the exercise to you. You may also record it in advance and play it back for yourself, or you may read it as you progress, taking as much time as you want.

You may begin by focusing on your breathing. Inhale and exhale slowly, and allow yourself to feel the peace and love of the Universe as you do so. With each breath, you may feel your muscles relax more and more. When you feel any particular muscle stiffen, just let it relax. Let your eyes go out of focus and slowly close as you begin to concentrate on your third eye.

Now you may feel the energy of your third eye begin to flow as it opens to the Golden Light of the Universe. You may feel the peace and love in total balance with your third-eye chakra. You may hear the tone of the energy as it finds its balance. Continue to breathe in and out slowly, and spend a few moments with the love and peace of your third eye as the Golden Light of the Universe gently encloses you in its protective cloak.

Balance Your Chakras

Now you may begin to work your way down through the rest of your chakras, focusing on your throat chakra next. You may feel the love and peace of the Universe flowing downward to and through your throat energy center. When you feel that this center is balanced, focus on your heart. Continue to repeat the opening and balancing exercise, on each chakra until you have opened and balanced your root chakra. After you have completed your balancing exercise, you may turn your focus back to your throat chakra, the source of your clairaudient abilities.

Listen to Your Mind

When you are ready, you may focus on your throat chakra and let your energy center open to any voice, sound, or music that flows through. At first there may be a lot of interference from outside sound stimuli or internal static from your conscious mind. All you need to do is relax and feel the love and peace of the Universe flow through your throat center. Just breathe in and out and let your mind wander. You may become aware of a distant voice, sound, or music. Just let it continue and focus on hearing it clearer and turning up the volume if needed.

Practice Pointer

Many composers hear their compositions in their head before they put them on paper. A composer might wake up in the middle of the night and write down what he just dreamed. Listen to your mind; who knows what you'll hear.

Identify Your Guides, Spirits, or Angels

You may ask that you hear the voice or voices of your guides, angels, or other spirits. There may be more than one guide, each of whom has a specific purpose in communicating with you. You may get an answer through your own internal voice, or you might hear other voices. You may hear the voice of a loved one who has passed over to the Other Side.

You can ask the name of the voice on the other end. It may be revealed to you, or you may come up with your own name. Do your voices have an agenda for you? If you have a question for the Universal Mind, your guides, or the angels, you may ask and turn it over for an appropriate answer. You may or may not get an answer right away. You may receive insights on world conditions, advice on health issues for others as well as for yourself, or spiritual messages that can help you grow in your knowledge of the Universe.

Keep a Record of Your Experiences

While you are in a relaxed state, ask yourself if there are any other kinds of internal clairaudience that you may receive. You may hear intuitive voices that may or may not make sense to you. Remember, you are the information gatherer at this point in your life map. Even though you may not understand it at the time you receive it, its purpose may become apparent in the future. You may hear the information more than once from both your internal and external sources. As you become more aware of your clairaudience, it is a good idea to keep notes of what you hear internally. You can write down an event after it happens—as soon as you can—making note of the time, date, and your mental, physical, and spiritual condition at the time. Also make note of each situation, including associations with other people, needs that you may have, and even locations and the regularity of your clairaudience.

Practice Pointer

Be prepared! Keep writing material close to your bed for insights that come in the night. You may even need a flashlight so you can see to make notes. When you travel, carry a small notepad or diary with you. If you choose to use a recording device to make your notes on, always carry a fresh set of batteries and extra tape.

You may find a special place, time, and technique that will provide you with the best and clearest psychic clairaudient experience. Once you have identified your best signal, anchor the state so that you can also use it in different locations. Give yourself a key word, phrase, or touch to help you connect with your psychic intuition. The more you practice, the easier it will be to enter your clairaudient state.

Hearing Things That Others Do Not

Now it's time to check your external clairaudience. When you actually hear voices, sounds, or music that others may not, it is often difficult to get anyone else to believe you really heard something that they didn't. It is always nice to have someone else verify what you have heard, but it is not necessary. The important thing is for you to feel comfortable with your psychic ability to hear more than most others do.

Because the external clairaudience experience can happen without warning, it is possible that sometimes it might catch you off guard. However, you should always remember that you can take your Belief, the Golden Light of the Universe, and your guides, angels, or other spirits with you wherever you go. You may always feel grounded and safe regardless of any voices, sounds, or music that you hear without warning.

Practice Pointer

Every day, especially the first thing in the morning, take the time to find a few moments to center yourself. If you allow yourself to feel in balance with your mind, body, and soul, you will be prepared for external clairaudience.

Sounds from the Past and Future

Can you visit a location and hear sounds that may have been made there some time before? If so, can you determine when the sounds were made and what was taking place at that time? Do you hear the same sounds at the same location at different times? Can you tell the mood of the sounds? Can you remember these sounds so that you can recall them at a later time?

Do you hear external voices, sounds, or music that relates to the future? If so, do you receive warnings, good news, or even sweepstake numbers? Can you identify the voices, sounds, or music you hear externally? Do they come to you at specific times, places, or locations? Does a voice ever speak to you "out of nowhere" to warn you of impending danger?

Sounds and Sights Come Together in Psychic Flow

Now it's time to combine your clairvoyant and clairaudient abilities to examine how they work together. If you're ready, you will experience your internal psychic seeing and hearing abilities first.

Find a comfortable place, and prepare yourself to experience your universal golden light trance. Take a deep breath and slowly exhale. Close your eyes, and focus on your third-eye chakra. You may allow yourself to open and balance your chakras, taking time to feel the positive, peaceful, and loving energy of the Universe.

Wrap yourself in a bubble of golden light from the Universe, and then focus on the psychic energy flow of your third-eye and throat energy centers. When you feel very comfortable and peaceful, you may ask your Belief to experience either a visual image or a sound in your mind that may help you in your psychic development. Be patient. At first the images may come slowly.

As you learn to "tune in" to your psychic flow, it will become easier and easier to connect. You may have a lot of conscious clutter that needs to be filtered out. You can accomplish this by just letting it come and go without trying to control it. If you resist or try to redirect your conscious clutter, you will wind up fighting it rather than stepping aside and letting it flow off into space.

Let any images you have become clearer and clearer with each breath you take. Can you see and hear your image at the same time? Can you change views or raise and lower the volume of the sounds you hear? Can you watch your images as if you were watching a movie or video? Can you replay or slow down or speed up your images?

Moving Through Time

Can you receive images in pictures and sound that relate to the future? If so, do they relate to you, to someone you know, or to a larger area? Can you be shown and told things that will be helpful to you and/or others in the future? Can you see and hear warnings through your internal images?

Can you experience images and sounds together that are from a different time in history? Perhaps the images are from a past-life memory. Can you project your mind back to a period of history and see and hear what it was like to be there? Can you remember these experiences and replay them later in your mind?

Switching to External Mode

Now it's time to combine external vision and hearing. Have you ever found yourself drifting off in your mind and experiencing a visual scene that is accompanied by sounds? Have you ever been in a specific location and flashed back to a different time period and heard and saw it as a reality? Are you able to see and hear spirits, angels, or other entities? If so, can any of these beings communicate with you?

Are there any other ways that you are intuitively able to hear and see images? If so, have you learned what these images mean? Are you afraid of them, or have you learned to rely on them for guidance? Can you remember the images after you have experienced them? Do you enjoy your contact with your psychic pictures and sounds?

As you learn how to balance and use your clairvoyant and clairaudient abilities, you will begin to rely on these abilities for insights and guidance in your work, relationships, and spiritual development, as well as in other aspects of your life. Be patient, and remember to stay grounded and protected. Like any other skill or talent, the more you use it, the more it is ready to work for you.

What's That Feeling?

Clairsentience means "clear feeling." Many people argue that "feeling" is the most important of the five senses, perhaps because it is most often combined with one or more of the other senses. Even by itself, it can provide a wealth of psychic information.

There are two different types of feelings—those experienced through touch and those experienced as emotion—and each type can be processed internally and externally. Both types of feelings may relate to the past, present, or future. They may come to you in dreams, during trances, through your mind, or through external touch. It can be very difficult for some people to differentiate clairsentience from their other senses.

You may be able to feel the emotions of others or the temperature of the weather in a past life. Edgar Cayce was able to project himself to a location he had never been before and report back on weather conditions. Sensing psychic feelings can often be problematic for those who absorb the feelings of others.

Practice Pointer

Gavin DeBecker has written a great book entitled *The Gift of Fear: Survivor Signals That Protect Us from Violence*. If you are interested in intuitive feelings, this might be a good book for you to read.

Intuitive Touch

Touch is a very powerful sense. When you touch something, it can unleash a flow of psychic images. You may feel repelled or drawn by people or items that you touch. You may be able to feel an aura or energy field around a person, a location, a plant, or an animal. A touch can create a peaceful and secure feeling or evoke anger.

Many intuitive healers get much of their information through touch. Just as you may be able to feel the pull of an underwater current, they can feel the current of energy as it flows through a body and can direct its movements with their hands.

There are many different ways that the sense of touch provides you with psychic information. It may be as simple as feeling an energy field around someone. It may be through the use of a dowsing rod or a pendulum when you feel the answer to a question you have asked the Universe. It may be that you can feel a tingle in your hands or a hum in your third eye when you are experiencing a psychic connection. As you are collecting information, you might feel a pain, an itch, a tickle, or a pulsating sensation.

You may have a psychic defense system that issues warnings or validations through certain feelings. Even though many originate in your mind, you still may actually feel them externally or physically. Learning how your body produces certain physical feelings that relate to psychic messages can be very helpful to you as you develop and become comfortable with your intuitive abilities.

The feeling of certain textures can produce psychic images as well. For instance, a certain food texture could trigger a past-life memory. The same thing is true for the texture of something you touch or wear. Textures can suddenly change your focus to the second image of a psychic hologram.

Feelings Evoked by Objects, Places, or People

Have you ever held or touched an object and gotten a feeling about its past? You may have been able to feel a mood through the object or something else about the people who have held it before. There is a belief that your energy is absorbed by anything you come in contact with. If you were affected by a strong mood during a time when you connected to an object, your mood or feelings would have been integrated into the object's energy. When you are open to this stored energy, you will receive an impression of its ownership history.

Have you ever been someplace and all of a sudden felt a very strong emotional feeling that was not related to your mood at the time? Have you ever had the feeling in certain locations that ghosts or spirits or something else was watching you? If so, what type of feelings did you have? Were they feelings of happiness, sadness, fear, peace, or something else? When you visit places where you have never been before, do you ever have the feeling that you are "home" again?

Can you think of someone and sense his mood or state of well-being at that time? Can you look into a person's eyes and feel the essence of her soul? Can you feel if the person is sincere or a potential threat? Have you ever met someone for the first time and felt as though the two of you have known each other for your whole lives? All of these feelings come through your psychic abilities of clairsentience.

Have you ever felt that your guides, angels, or something else was protecting you? If so, how do you get this feeling? Can you create a feeling that you are being protected when you need or want that feeling? Do you have a technique that you use everyday to surround yourself with Universal Protection? If so, how does your feeling help you?

Figure Out Your Feeling for Others

Do you absorb feelings and/or emotions from other people, places, or objects? If you do, how do you respond to what you feel? The intuitive ability to feel is a wonderful gift. But it can also be a terrible curse. For those who are extremely open to clairsentience, it's as if feelings have the power to penetrate the very essence of their souls. This statement is true of many artists and healers.

A PSYCHIC TRUTH

Many first-time students of massage, Reiki, or nursing have a great deal of trouble in dealing with the physical, mental, and spiritual pain of their clients and patients. The students are absorbers, suddenly thrust into the unbalanced energy of those they are trying to heal. If you are learning hands-on healing arts such as massage or Reiki, it is a good idea to ground yourself often.

If You Have the Gift

Your psychic gift may be the ability to experience the mental, physical, and spiritual makeup of other people, locations, time periods, and all other things living now or in the past. Once you have absorbed any of these feelings, they become part of your energy. The feelings will continue to stay with you unless you are able to release them.

Any energy you absorb, positive or negative, can impact your own energy as long as it remains with you in the form it was received. If the energy is positive, it can have a positive effect on your total energy. But if the energy is negative, it can have a negative effect on your total energy.

If you are an energy absorber, you are not alone. Many other people do the same thing. You always look for the good, and it seems as if all you receive is the bad. Yet your natural ability is to care and to absorb. It's okay to care and absorb, and it's also okay—in fact, it's even better—to turn the concerns and negative energy over to your Universal Team to help resolve and purify.

If you are an absorber, you may allow yourself to let the negative energy pass through you and out into the Universe for cleansing and healing. You need not be affected by the energy that is going through you.

Physical Feelings of Emotions

Do you ever get an emotional feeling that changes into a physical feeling? Perhaps the hair stands up on the back of your neck or you feel a pain in your neck. Your head might buzz, or you may feel a sudden heaviness in your stomach. Your knees might get weak, or perhaps you get a pain someplace in your body. Perhaps you experience some other kind of cue that lets you know that something is not right.

Sadness can cause you to feel heaviness in your heart center. Your third-eye chakra may respond to your aura being invaded by someone else's energy. If you are grounded, you may be able to actually feel your protective shield or the bubble of golden light deflecting off the unwanted attempt to take over your space.

Not all transferences of emotional feelings are to warn you of bad news. You may get a body feeling that validates to you that something psychic is taking place at that moment. You may feel a buzz of psychic energy in one or more of your chakras. You may get a special feeling when someone is thinking positive thoughts about you. There are many ways in which you can transfer an emotional image into a physical feeling.

How Does Your Energy Fit into the Universe?

Part of clairsentience is being able to manipulate the energy of the Universe. Can you receive Universal Energy and then project it into someone else's aura or body for the purpose of healing? Some of you may be able to bring the strength of the Universe through you rather than absorbing the negative energy from someone or something else. Do others find that you have a calming or healing effect when you touch them? Can you smooth out the energy in the auras of other people? If so, you may be a natural healer.

Is your energy so strong that it affects others without your even realizing it? Do you have trouble keeping wristwatches running? Do you have trouble with your electric appliances, computers, or other electronic items? If so, you may be emitting a very strong psychic energy field with the power to affect sensitive equipment.

Can you produce extra strength to move objects when you need to? Do you have the ability to move objects with your mind or by sending an energy field through your fingers? Many of you may have special strengths that are part of your psychic energy. If you have that gift, you have an opportunity to do a lot of good with your "power" from the Universe.

Protect Your Heart Chakra

The energy connected to your clairsentient powers is located in the heart chakra. When the heart chakra is open, you are open to the emotional energy of many different sources. You may receive clairsentience from other people, animals, plants, objects, locations, time periods, ghosts, those on the Other Side, and forms of energy.

If your heart chakra is out of balance, you can receive too much feeling energy, or you might even absorb negative auras into your own aura. If your heart center is blocked, you will receive or be aware of very little emotion.

A PSYCHIC TRUTH

Protection for your clairsentience is extremely important. When your heart chakra is open and unbalanced, you could be over-whelmed with external emotional and internal feelings. They can come from people, locations, dreams, past lives, future events, ghosts, or deceased spirits.

Creative abilities are often the most powerful when the chakra centers are open. At those times, artists, writers, musicians, or dancers produce and/or perform their greatest work. When they are caught up in the energy flow, they are in a state in which their conscious minds are not fully aware of what is taking place. They can only focus on the creative flow until it has run its course. These trance states may last a short time or may go on for days, placing the artist at risk of losing touch with reality.

When the centers close up again, the creative effort may or may not be complete. If the results are unfinished, there is always the possibility that the centers will not open again. If the work is complete, there may be a chance that the chakras will remain closed and that there will be no more works of that kind produced again. It is the ego mind that causes the doubt, not the intuitive trance. If you are balanced, the flow is natural. The creative energy will always be there in its own way, which will always be the cor-rect way for that moment in time.

A Chakra-Balancing Exercise

You may open and balance your heart chakra using the chakra-balancing exercise. Find a comfortable place to relax and focus on your breathing. Begin by connecting to your third-eye chakra, and ask your Universal Power to bring down its loving, peaceful positive energy.

Include the protective bubble of universal golden light and let it flow over and around you.

When you are ready, let yourself open and balance each chakra, beginning with your third eye and on downward until you release the kundalini energy to mix with the peace and love of the Universe. Now let yourself be aware that your crown chakra is open and balanced and ready to receive the proper clairsentience that is right for you at this time. Allow yourself to focus on your heart chakra.

Investigate Your Clairsentience

From your relaxed state, with your focus on your heart chakra, you may begin to investigate the particular manner in which you receive your intuitive feelings and how you can develop and use them. Do you feel emotions? If so, what kind of emotions do you feel? Can you feel the moods of other people or animals? Can you feel the moods of specific locations or from objects?

Can you feel the moods of spirits of beings who may have died and left unresolved issues on the earth plane? Do you feel emotions about certain events in a different period of history or about the future? Are you overwhelmed with emotions at certain times and don't know why? Do you feel the emotions of family or friends with whom you do not have daily contact? Do you ever get a "gut feeling" that you should contact someone immediately?

The Joining of the Psychic Senses

Once you gain some understanding of your clairsentient abilities, you can then work to merge them with your other senses. First, let's combine your feeling sense with vision and hearing. As you do so, you will become aware of how these three senses work for you and how they can be used in your psychic development.

When you are ready, you may get comfortable and focus on your breathing. Next focus on your third-eye chakra and feel yourself connecting to a loving and peaceful flow of Universal Energy. Now you may open and balance your chakras as you feel the protective bubble of golden universal light totally covering you.

Continue to focus on your third eye, and then add in your throat and your heart chakras. When you are ready, ask your Universal Power that you may see, hear, and feel the psychic information that is right for you at this moment in time. If you have a specific question for the Universe, your guides, or your angels, you may ask it at this time and give permission for the answer to come when it is ready to be received. You may give yourself a few moments to let the images form in your mind.

Add the Senses of Taste and Smell

In addition to sight, hearing, and feeling, you may also use your senses of taste and smell to help produce your psychic images. It is now time to add them to your intuitive assessment exercise. Some of you will get powerful images through smell. The smells you sense may come to you as a communication from the Other Side, or you may experience a smell from a different period of time when you visit certain locations. Whenever you are receiving psychic information, pay attention to which one or more of your senses are gathering the information.

As you remain in the trance, ask yourself the following questions. Do certain tastes or smells evoke psychic images? Do these images relate to past lives or future events? Or can you experience something that is taking place in present time, simultaneously though in a different location? Do you ever have visions? If so, in which one or more of the five senses do you experience them?

Can you visit a location and experience it in a different period of time, using all five of your senses? Can you see, hear, feel, taste, or smell what took place there before or what will take place there in the future? Can you project to a different location and experience with all your five senses what is happening at the same moment? Can you communicate using your mind with someone who is not with you physically?

Practice Pointer

If you feel overwhelmed emotionally and are having trouble finding a balance in your life, you should seek out a qualified counselor in your area. Sometimes a person forgets how to close an open channel once it is open, and in that case it is advisable to get some help.

Can you see, feel, hear, or smell other spirits? Do your guides, angels, or other spirits have a particular scent? Which one or more of your senses are the strongest and most reliable at experiencing psychic external images? Which sense is the weakest? Are there any other types of psychic images that you experience that could be developed for positive use and to help guide you along your life map?

Anchor Your Psychic Self

You have now engaged your five different senses in imagery designed to help you identify your psychic gifts. The more you can identify your strengths, the more useful they will be in the rest of this book as you examine specific psychic functions. You may be strong in all of them or strong in some of them.

When you are in your relaxed state, with your chakras in balance, give yourself a key word or touch that will help you bring back your intuitive state. The more you can enter a safe and protected intuitive trance, the more you will maintain your balance. It is okay to carry your bubble with you.

Beware of Misusing Your Gifts

The goal as you develop your psychic gifts is to understand what your ability is and to become comfortable in engaging it. Remember, no one on earth is just like you. No one has your special psychic abilities.

However, there are people who use their psychic gifts for their own selfish gain. They are very good at identifying absorbers, for instance, and taking full advantage of them to satisfy their egos. They have a need to control with their psychic powers. But what they don't realize is that the power they wield is not their own but the power of the Universe. They may possess what seems to others great power and control in their current lifetime, but they may be out of tune with their life purpose. It is inevitable that they will have to settle the score with their karmas sometime in the future. Beware of these psychic predators who feed on the unsuspecting, leaving a wake of confusion and self-doubt in those whom they successfully dominate.

Dreams as Psychic Mediums

Dreams are a great medium for receiving psychic information. They come at a time when your conscious mind is at rest and open to the messages of your unconscious and your Universal Mind. Because your conscious mind is so active, many of you do not relax enough while you are awake to receive the information that is there for you. At night, you may have many dreams, but most of them go unnoticed. Even if you are aware of having dreamt when you wake up, you may quickly forget the contents of those dreams.

Practice Pointer

If you dream of something more than once, pay attention. Many psychic dreams are given to you for a specific reason. They may concern your health, safety, or even career choice.

Dream Recall

When you prepare for bed, make an entry into your dream journal—you can also use a tape recorder. Make sure the listing includes the time, what you last ate, and when and how you feel mentally, physically, and spiritually. If you have a request for your guides, angels, higher power, or just for the Universe, ask that an answer may come in your dreams.

Then, when you awake, make sure that you record your dreams as you remember them. Include as many details about your dream as you can remember—the type of dream, theme, people, places, time period, and whether you have had this or similar dreams before.

Dream Patterns

Even if you wake with no conscious memory of a dream, make a note in your journal about how you feel. Over a period of time, the data you collect will help you establish your sleep and dream patterns. Do your dreams occur regularly or sporadically? Do you remember dreams daily, weekly, monthly, or less often than that? Do you have specific dreams for specific moments in your life? Do you dream more when you eat certain foods before you go to bed?

The following sections will help you distinguish between various types of psychic dreams, including dreams that have to do with your past lives, dreams concerning the future, and symbolic dreams.

Unfinished Business Reappears

One type of dream that often starts in childhood and may or may not continue into adulthood are dreams that deal with a past life.

Children may not recognize that what they are dreaming is from a past life, but they may notice that in their dream, they and their family members appear in different roles.

A past-life dream is set during a different time period. The dream may be repetitious and have a theme that was imprinted in the soul of the past life. It's not unusual for the past-life dream to be traumatic—many of these dreams are nightmares. For example, a past-life dream may be an event that led up to a death scene, with the dream ending before the actual event. Upon waking, the feeling of terror lingers.

A Psychic Truth

Past-life dreams are often karmic in nature. In other words, your dream may relate to unfinished business from a previous lifetime. The dream may give you a clue as to how you can resolve the karma in your current lifetime. It is possible to use a past-life dream as the catalyst to go deeper into the past life through the technique of hypnosis.

Look for Clues

Here is how you can figure out whether a particular dream is giving you clues or revealing episodes concerning your past life. Often, these dreams have visual images that you recognize. Does the dream's location seem familiar and yet as though it doesn't belong to your lifetime? Sometimes that distinction is easy to make, and sometimes it is not. A child may not recognize the difference of a few years, whereas an adult would. Also, if the turnaround time between incarnations is short, the child may blend his or her current life with the one that he or she experiences just previously.

If there are people in the dream, how are they dressed? Are they wearing modern clothes? Can you see yourself in the dream, or are you only experiencing it? If you cannot see yourself, hypnosis may help you get more information about who the characters in your dream may have been.

Is there anything else that may give you a clue about the possibility of a past-life dream? You may awake from a past-life dream with an emotion that connects to another lifetime. What other clues would you collect from a dream to imply that it may have been about your past lives?

Dreams of Flight

A subset of past-life dreams are flying dreams. Have you ever dreamed that you are able to soar in the sky, as free as a bird? Some people believe that dreams of flying date back to the earliest reincarnations of your soul because they go back to a time when you had no physical form. At that time you were able to travel using the pure energy of thought as your power. Dreams give your soul a chance to fly again without the constraints of your physical, human body.

Do you fly in any of your dreams? If so, where do you go? Do you travel to other worlds or to heavenly realms? Do you fly backward or forward in time? Where else do you fly? Do you fly alone or with others? Can you choose a destination before you go to sleep and fly there during a dream? Do you ever dream about falling or floating? Is there a pattern to these dreams? Exploring the answers to these questions is an important part of developing your psychic ability.

Predictions and Insight about the Future

Do you have dreams about events that have not happened yet? Many of the great prophets throughout history have relied on their dreams to provide the insights that helped rulers make their decisions about the future. These predictions included floods, famines, and other weather changes. They also included predictions of wars and threats to the people, the land, and even to the rulers themselves.

When you are out of balance and your energy centers are open, you are susceptible to receiving psychic images from the Universe. These images include events that have not yet happened. When you go to sleep in a state of confusion and out of balance, your dreams become a conduit for images of the future. Unfortunately many of these types of dreams are not happy, but tragic.

Good and Bad

Is there a pattern to your prophetic dreams? Do you dream of winning numbers in the lottery before they are drawn? Do you dream about questions and answers on tests before you take them? Do you dream of meeting people and then actually meet them?

Do you dream of future events? If so, are these related to your life and the lives of others you know? Are your dreams about events that may take place on a worldwide scale? Do you dream of disasters before they happen, such as plane crashes, assassinations of famous people, or wars? How often do you have this type of dream?

A Psychic Truth

Prophetic dreams may be messages from your guides, angels, or other forms of higher power. They are often given to you as a warning for the future. Listen to yourself after you have a prophetic dream. Your psychic intuition will indicate how you should respond.

How do you feel during and after you have a prophetic dream? Do you feel helpless, or are you compelled to take action as a result of your dream? Where do you think your prophetic dreams are coming from? Do you wish that you could block out this type of dream? What else do you experience when you have a dream about the future?

Look for Symbols and Sequences

Once in a while, you will experience a dream that feels like a riddle. It may involve snippets and pieces of events in your life, usually close in time to when the dream is experienced. These snippets may be from news accounts, or they may come from some memory in your unconscious mind. These pieces are woven into the dream theme but are out of character with the actual events.

Symbolic dreams may come in sequences or segments. They may be experienced over several different nights or weeks. The dreams can relate to you or to events that are taking place in the world. Dream themes can deal with events that have happened or with events that have yet to happen.

Symbolic dreams are easily dismissed as nonsense dreams. These are dreams that are often attributed to too much rich food or experiences you might have lived through earlier in the day. Even when a dream seems to make no sense, make a note of it in your dream journal, and you may find a pattern developing in your symbolic dreams.

Make Attempts at Interpretation

To help you identify a dream that has symbolic content, note the apparent theme of the dream. Is it repeated in the dream? Do you have the same dream or a series of different dreams with the same recurring theme? Are there people, animals, or other beings in your symbolic dreams?

Do you have houses or rooms of a house in your dreams? How do the dreams make you feel? Can you hear voices or other sounds? Do the actions in the dreams make any sense to you at first review? What else can you note from your dreams that may be considered symbolic?

Practice Pointer

Analysis of a symbolic dream can be complicated due to the subject material and how it relates to you. Try to record as much information as soon as possible in your dream journal. Someone else, or a book on dreams, may provide a clue as to what and why you dreamed it.

Tarot Tells All

Even though symbols used in tarot cards may have come to us from the ancient cultures of Egypt, Greece, Rome, and China, the origins of the Tarot deck and its use in divination are much more recent. According to the International Tarot Society, Tarot comes from northern Italy, where it was introduced sometime between 1420 and 1440. At first, the Tarot was just a new type of card game, similar to bridge, which was played by the upper class in Italy and France.

The tarot cards were handcrafted and elaborately illustrated. As the game became more popular and spread, each artist would add to or change the illustrations according to his cultural interests. Today, early tarot decks are highly prized by collectors because these works of art are windows through which you can view the history of the time period when the cards were made.

A PSYCHIC TRUTH

When you receive a Tarot reading from a psychic, the cards themselves act as tools to help the reader create intuitive images that relate to your life. The psychic may get internal information from his or her guidance system in one or more of the five senses.

A. E. Waite standardized the tarot deck to include seventy-eight cards, divided into the Major Arcana and Minor Arcana. The Major Arcana is comprised of twenty-two thematic trump cards that represent archetypal forces in your life. With the exception of the Fool, each card in the Major Arcana is assigned a number. The Minor Arcana includes fifty-six cards subdivided into four suits: cups, swords, wands, and pentacles (originally, wands were polo sticks and pentacles were coins). Each of the suits contains ace through ten, plus page, knight, queen, and king. The cards of the Minor Arcana can help you focus on your direction in your life journey.

Using Tarot in Divination

Tarot is no longer played like a game of cards as it was originally. The deck is now mainly used as a tool to forecast the future. At first, learning to read the Tarot may seem like an insurmountable task. That's why there are professional readers who can interpret the cards for you. The reader's job is really to help you become aware of your life's direction and of the positive and negative outcomes as you continue your journey.

If you decide that you want to use the Tarot to enhance your psychic abilities, you should try different decks to see which one feels right for you. It may be that you relate to particular images, or perhaps you'll get certain psychic sensory clues that are evoked by a certain sense. Consider your other spiritual interests—you may relate to nature, to particular symbols, or to Native American imagery. What you are looking for is a set that will resonate with your psyche.

Tarot is a very interesting form of psychic power. To learn more about the decks, spreads, and readings, you can check out *The Everything® Tarot Book, 2nd Edition* by Skye Alexander.

Astrological Bodies Affect Human Potential

Astrology is a form of divination. It is based on the belief that the movement of celestial bodies affects human potential and other events on earth just as the moon directly influences the rise and fall of the ocean tides. Over the years, elaborate systems have been developed to correlate predictions of future events through the movement of these heavenly bodies. More than one system of astrology has developed. For instance, Chinese astrology is based on the phases of the moon.

> A PSYCHIC TRUTH
> Each of the astrological signs contains one of four elements. These elements are fire (Aries, Leo, and Sagittarius), air (Gemini, Libra, and Aquarius), water (Cancer, Scorpio, and Pisces), and earth (Taurus, Virgo, and Capricorn).

One of astrology's central concepts is that because the soul is reborn at a specific time in relationship to the positions of the planets, its destiny as it journeys through its life plane is in direct relationship to the movements of celestial bodies. If you are aware of your position on earth in relationship to the stars, you have a better opportunity to be aware of your potential karmic gains and losses as you progress through your life map.

Twelve Houses of Destiny

The most popular type of astrology today relies on the position of the sun at the time of birth to predict events in each person's future as well. Through the course of the year, the sun travels through twelve houses of the zodiac:

* Aries: March 21–April 19
* Taurus: April 20–May 20
* Gemini: May 21–June 20
* Cancer: June 21–July 22
* Leo: July 23–August 22
* Virgo: August 23–September 22
* Libra: September 23–October 22
* Scorpio: October 23–November 21
* Sagittarius: November 22–December 21

* Capricorn: December 22–January 19
* Aquarius: January 20–February 18
* Pisces: February 19–March 20

Each of the twelve signs has its own personality traits. Since you were born under a specific sign, you are expected to exhibit the personality traits of that sign. As you delve into the science of astrology, you will read about personality profiles and compatibility of the different birth signs. If you have a strong relationship with someone who has an incompatible birth sign, remember that you can help make the relationship better. Don't just abandon it.

Your Personalized Horoscope Reading

The daily positions of the planets affect each sun sign. To learn what to expect on a daily basis, many people rely on their horoscopes. Horoscopes are posted daily and are available online, in newspapers, and even on radio programs. These are general, and they apply to people according to their sun sign. Some people won't make a move until they find out what the stars say that day.

A more detailed horoscope, also known as a birth chart, is a map of the heavenly bodies as it appeared at the time of your birth. Usually, it appears in the shape of a wheel and is filled with symbols, or glyphs, for your sun and moon signs. A good astrologer has the ability to interpret the symbols to help you understand the potential meaning of your birth chart. With the astrologer's help, you can begin to use your horoscope as a guide to the future.

When an astrologer prepares your personal horoscope, he is relying on information that is based on hundreds of years of data that has been refined over time. Once you have acquired your own chart, you are free to use the information as you wish.

9

PSYCHIC TOOLBOX

Scrying to Peer into the Future

Scrying is a form of divination. Its name comes from the word "to descry"—to make out dimly. Scrying is usually done for the specific purpose of peering into the future. This may be done through a number of different tools. Reading a crystal ball, the smoke of a candle, or oil poured on water are all forms of visual scrying; however, any of the five senses may be used.

Scyring is actually a way of entering into a trance state. As you stare at an object and let your eyes go out of focus, a second image (a hologram) begins to appear. As you focus on the hologram, you step into a different time zone. Usually, scrying is used to see the future, but it is also possible to use scrying methods for visiting the past. As long as you focus on the second image, you will stay in your psychic trance, and when you shift back to the reality of the moment, you will return to your normal state.

Other forms of divination require that you manipulate a physical object and then enter your trance state to interpret the patterns formed by your actions. Examples of this include the casting of runes or I Ching coins. Once these items are cast, the psychic uses the unconscious mind to make interpretations of the patterns they make, seeing what possibilities the future may hold in store.

A PSYCHIC TRUTH

When you select a tool that can potentially enhance your psychic ability, make sure that it is in tune with your energy. Sometimes people try to use an aid that is not right for them, which can result in loss of confidence in their psychic power.

Identify and Use Your Psychic Tools

Before you begin to work with a tool, always let your energy balance and become in tune with universal love and peace. Take a few moments and center yourself. Use your self-hypnosis anchors to help you feel the protection of a golden bubble of universal light surrounding and filling you with peace and love. Ask your Universal Power that you may experience something positive from the tool you are experimenting with to help you become more in tune with your life map and soul's purpose.

While you are in a relaxed and connected intuitive state, let yourself open up to both your internal and external guidance systems. Internally, ask that the images may come through in one or more of your senses that work best for you. Ask that your external team reaffirm what your internal guidance already knows. Then let yourself be aware of the affirmations that may come to you.

A psychic tool should have the right feel. Just like rediscovering a soul mate, a psychic tool may be one that you are also finding again for the first time in this life. You may come across an implement that feels as comfortable as an old shoe. The next step is learning to trust it once more. Once you have found your old friend again, keep it with you as you continue your psychic development.

The Crystal Ball, Not What You May Think

When you think of a gypsy fortuneteller, chances are you imagine a woman in mystic clothing peering into a crystal ball in a dimly lit room. As she gazes into the sphere, she begins to see a glimpse of your future. She seems to go into some sort of a spell as she continues her monologue in her monotonous voice. You may wonder how it is that this magical crystal ball holds the information of your soul.

The crystal ball helps you go into your psychic trance. To try it, center on the ball, letting your eyes go out of focus, and ask your guidance system to provide you with the proper images for the information that you are asking from your Universal Mind. The more you practice and pay attention to your natural psychic intuition, the more you will be able to define the type of crystal ball that may be right for you.

Choose Your Crystal

Crystal balls come in various sizes and in a wide range of prices. Some can cost over a thousand dollars or even more, depending on the material they are made of. For some of you, the energy in rock crystals—those made of natural stone—corresponds with your psychic vibrational frequencies. In other words, the crystal may help open your psychic energy centers and make your intuitive connection stronger. If, on the other hand, your frequency and that of the crystal ball are out of sync, it may interfere with your natural psychic ability.

A Psychic Truth

A natural rock crystal is generally composed of a clear piece of quartz or beryl. It is believed that these substances contain magnetic properties that can help amplify your body's own energy field. The combination of the two energies is thought to help your connection to your soul and your ability to use your psychic gifts.

Different kinds of rock crystal have different vibrational levels. The best way to find out which is right for you is to go to a store that sells several kinds of rock crystal balls so that you can compare how they resonate with your vibrational level. If you are not affected by the energy in rock crystals, you may want to look at other types of crystal balls, such as those made of glass or Lucite.

Your perfect crystal might not be a crystal at all. You might find a different type of stone that contains the right energy. You could even use a piece of metal, wood, or coral to help you get into your psychic trance zone. If you are sensitive to energy, the more you learn to work with it, the more in balance your psychic vibrations will be.

Energy Emanating Rocks and Runes

Some of you might enjoy collecting special stones that you can cast in patterns that may help produce psychic images. These stones could be from the ocean or the mountains. They may come from the same place or from many different locations. The more compatible the stones' energies are with yours, the more productive the readings will become.

Once you've got a set of stones, you can begin developing a pattern in casting your stones. You could read them on the first throw or the second or the third. If you are not sure how many times you should cast the stones before reading their patterns, ask your unconscious mind for some guidance.

Practice Pointer
You may want to begin collecting stones that have special meaning to you. Look for the right stones by placing your hands over them to see if you get a special feeling; you can also sit nearby and feel the energies emanating from them.

The Energy of the Stones

Feeling the energy of a stone or a group of stones may help induce a psychic trance. To try this, select some stones that have positive vibrations for you. You can hold them in your hands as you let your eyes go out of focus and enter your intuitive trance state. Now focus on the positive energy of the stones and ask that the right images be given you to provide answers to your questions.

You can also look for a large boulder and use its powerful energy to go into a trance. Find one that you can sit on, and try communicating with it. As you do, remember to always allow yourself to be grounded and protected in your golden bubble of light of the Universal Mind.

Casting Runes

Runes are ancient Norse symbols carved on small rocks or tiles. When a diviner casts runes, she can use the symbols to interpret the results in order to get answers to questions about the future. Make sure that the set of runes you select has an accompanying booklet that explains the meanings of the symbols and helps guide you on how to find the answers to your questions. Casting methods vary. You can select a single rune tile from a bag, cast them in lots, or place them in patterns as some people do with tarot cards.

Ancient Form of Fortunetelling, Tea Leaves

Another psychic tool that is associated with gypsy fortunetelling is tea leaves. If you would like to try reading tea leaves, brew yourself a pot using loose-leaf tea. Pour a cup, and let the tea leaves settle. As you drink the tea, communicate with your Belief. Consider your goals for the reading, and prepare to read the patterns in the leaves after you finish.

A PSYCHIC TRUTH

Gazing into a bowl of dark liquid is one of the oldest forms of psychic foretelling. Early rituals included the use of blood and even the entrails of freshly sacrificed animals to help create an intuitive trance state.

Here is a routine that you may want to try. After you finish your cup of tea, slowly turn the cup upside down and let any remaining liquid drain out into the saucer. Then, twirl the cup around three times, and turn it right-side up again. Now, you can gaze into the tea leaves left in the bottom of the cup and intuitively read the patterns they formed.

If you try this, be sure to use a kind of tea that you enjoy and that is also relaxing. Let your eyes go out of focus, and let the information flow up to the surface of your conscious mind. If you find this method potentially helpful, you will want to develop your own ritual for focusing.

Connect to the Other Side with a Ouija Board

The Ouija board is one of the more controversial kinds of psychic tools. This is largely due to the belief that the players are contacting dead spirits or other entities from the Other Side who help guide the participants' hands over the board as a means of communication. Many Christians believe that those who use the Ouija board are communicating with the devil. Others believe that it is only the players' unconscious minds that are providing the answers.

Practice Pointer

If you use the Ouija board, always make sure that you are very grounded and protected by the Golden Light of the Universe. Many people have played the game for fun, only to find out that the Other Side is very serious.

The word "Ouija" is a combination of *oui* and *ja,* the words for "yes" in French and German. The game board includes all the letters of the alphabet and the numbers zero through nine, plus the words "yes," "no," and "goodbye." The roots of Ouija go back to ancient China, but it was Elijah Bond who created the current game in 1892. Ouija boards became very popular after World War I, when relatives of soldiers who died in the war would make an attempt to contact them through the Ouija board.

To use the Ouija board, two or more players place their fingertips on a heart-shaped planchette that has three felt-tipped legs. The planchette glides over the surface of the board and spells out the answers to the question asked. Sometimes the spirits have a mind of their own and take over the game.

Lines and Patterns in Palmistry

The ancient art of telling your future by reading your palms is thought to have originated in China or India as early as 3000 B.C. In Europe, it was practiced by witches and gypsies, and its popularity rose in the late nineteenth century as the public became more interested in spiritualism and the occult.

According to palmistry, the shape of your hands carries information about your physical and artistic traits. Lines, creases, and bumps found on the palms contain information about the past events of your life as well as the future; there is also information about your life map and soul's purpose. Some readers compare palmistry with astrology. They look for a relationship formed in the patterns in your palms to the signs of the zodiac.

A PSYCHIC TRUTH
If you are right-handed, your left hand indicates your life map while

your right hand reveals how you have followed your soul's purpose. If you are left-handed, the roles of your hands are reversed.

Changing the Patterns

The lines and markings in your palms may actually change over time to reflect the changes in your life. However, you can also actively work to change your palm patterns—thus changing the potential of your future—through the practice of Zen or yoga. Both of these practices, and yoga in particular, are spiritual belief systems that seek to liberate the spirit from physical matter for the purpose of becoming one with the Universal Mind.

Use Your Senses as Tools, Too

It's fun to cast runes, look into coffee grounds, or try your hand at the crystal ball, but you don't need fancy paraphernalia to work with your psychic powers. Your senses can be effective tools as well—see if you can rely on sounds, smells, touching, or emotions to gather psychic information.

Playing by Ear

Sound can be a very important element in helping to create a psychic trance. Try playing soft music in the background, or get a small fountain, sit by a stream or the ocean, and listen! Another alternative is to use a recording of natural sounds. The sound of drums, bells, or chimes is also an effective way to put yourself in touch with your intuitive mind. Even a verbalized tone, such as chanting or humming "om," can help.

An Emotional Connection

You can also try to establish an emotional connection; for instance, you could visit a place that has certain meaning for you. If your emotion is deep, it can help you enter a trance state. Maybe you feel deep calm when you visit a special place in the woods, or when you come to the beach. You could have special associations with visiting a church, synagogue, or temple, especially if these places can put you closer in touch with your Belief System. For some people, the simple action of staring at the full moon will give them a feeling that they can use psychically.

> ### A Psychic Truth
>
> Many cultures use sound to help induce trance states. Australian Aborigines use the didgeridoo to produce a constant drone. Native Americans and Africans use drumbeats. Tibetans use bells and horns to help establish connections to the Universal Mind.

Special Scents

Certain smells may also help induce a trance—it's common to use incense, a candle with a special fragrance, fragrant oils, or herbs. You might want to burn some sage as a way of clearing old energies out of your present location.

Even a memory of a particular smell may affect you deeply enough to induce the trance state. Whenever you want to connect, take a deep breath and experience the feeling of something special.

The Magic Touch

The touch or feel of an object, such as a stone or perhaps something old that already has the experience of ancient wisdom in its energy, can help produce a psychic trance. It could be the clothes you choose to wear, the temperature of the room, a baby's blanket, or a piece of soft fleece—any such object may create the right feel to help you enter a trance.

Practice Pointer

Whenever you open your psychic abilities in order to receive information about the future, make sure you know what you are requesting. If you are not sure right from the very beginning, you may open yourself to knowledge that is not necessary for you to know at the current time.

Create Your Own Method

Once you try out various sensory techniques described here, you can go ahead and create your own method. For a moment, let yourself go into your relaxed trance state and think back over your life to times, places, and/or events that induced you into a spontaneous trance. It might have been a time when you looked into a steamy mirror after stepping out of a bath or shower. You were already in a relaxed state, and as you looked into the unclear image in front of you, your eyes suddenly saw something entirely different. It might have been on a foggy night when something seemed to materialize out of the mist.

It might have been a sound that induced you into a state of trance, such as the monotonous drone of an engine or a machine. It could have been the sound of many voices talking at once. It could have been while you were listening to a certain piece of music. It could have been an emotion that suddenly took over your conscious mind. As you think back, let your unconscious mind release your memories to you.

You may get an idea that you had not considered before. Make a note to try it out for helping you enter and enhance your psychic trance state. Some ideas may come to you later on in either a waking or a dream state. Once you have opened yourself to the possibility that you already have used naturally psychic tools in the past, all you have to do is wait for your internal and external guidance systems to remind you of them. These reminders may come from outside of yourself, so be aware at all times.

You may even have knowledge of psychic tools that are waiting in your unconscious mind from a past life. Now is the time to let them be updated to your present lifetime so that they may be used again to help you become and stay in tune with your life map. If you believe that you are letting your intuitive gifts be used for the greater good of others, you will be amazed at how you will become confident in and learn to rely on your own special psychic gifts. They are already there, no matter what tools you decide to work with.

10

Alternative Psychic Healing Methods

Faith healers have been a part of many cultures for millennia. Witch doctors, shamans, and medicine men, among others, played important roles in the societies they lived in. Jesus Christ was hailed as a great healer.

As late as the nineteenth century, magnetism and other methods of alternative healing enjoyed popularity, but many of the ancient healing arts eventually gave way to modern medicine. In fact, with the rise of modern medicine, the popularity of the old way of healing almost disappeared.

Edgar Cayce and the Healing Arts Revival

It was Edgar Cayce who unwittingly became the focal point of the New Age movement, which swept the country during the latter part of the twentieth century. Cayce's uncanny psychic ability to retrieve old healing remedies from the Akashic Records stored deep in the Universe changed the views of alternative medicine for many doubters.

While in a deep self-hypnotic trance, Cayce was able to scan a body with his mind and give a diagnosis based on what he saw. The subject did not even have to be in the same room for Cayce to be able to scan her body and give a diagnosis and recommend treatment for the affliction. The language that Cayce used in a trance was not the lingo or jargon of modern medicine. The treatments were given in terms that employed remedies long since forgotten. The diagnosis and treatments often focused on the body's energy system.

> ### A Psychic Truth
> If you are interested in getting more information on Edgar Cayce, you can go to the ARE Web site at *www.edgarcayce.org*. ARE is the Association for Research and Enlightenment located in Virginia Beach, Virginia. It was founded in 1931 and is still growing in membership today.

Many of you have Edgar Cayce's potential to psychically read the health of others and help facilitate their healing. Each one of you will do it a little differently. You will have the opportunity to consider several concepts of psychic healing in this chapter.

Positive Energy Fields and Understanding Auras

As you have already learned, your body is an energy grid. You have many energy centers, including your seven major chakras. When the energy is flowing evenly and all your centers are in balance, you are in tune mentally, physically, and spiritually with yourself and the Universal Energy. Your three minds are all working together in harmony with your Belief System and your guidance team. You are always connected to your third eye and completely immersed in a golden bubble of universal peace and love.

A Psychic Truth

Just about everyone has the ability to sense auras one way or another. If you are not aware of how you do it, you may not be paying attention to the clues you are giving yourself. Look for signals from your unconscious and your Universal Mind, and pay attention to your guidance systems.

Needless to say, to stay in this situation all the time is impossible. You are always being thrown off balance by life's resistances, both small and large. How soon you regain your balance and keep yourself in positive energy can have a direct outcome on your own wellness. When positive energy flow is blocked, negative energy can manifest itself through a weakness in your body, usually causing illness.

The flow of positive energy is what creates an energy field known as an aura. The more out of balance you are, the more your aura will be out of balance as well. That balance can be affected from moment to moment, and it is also influenced by the way you have taken care of yourself over a long period of time. The longer your aura remains unbalanced, the more susceptible you are to minor and major illnesses.

Reading an Aura

Each of you will read auras a little differently. Your mental makeup will help indicate how you will best experience an aura reading. If you have a strong visual sense, you may be able to see it. If you have a strong hearing sense, you may hear—either by voice or by other sounds—the energy of the aura. If you are sensitive to touch, you may feel an aura. If you have a strong sense of smell, you may smell the aura, and if you have a strong sense of taste, you may actually taste it. Some people may be able to use all of their senses, while others rely on two or more that combine to provide them with the image. A feeling may create a picture, or a smell may produce a feeling.

Your first step is to identify how you read an aura. Once you've figured that out, the next step is to collect the information you receive. What does it mean? When you read someone's aura, can you use the information to develop a model of his health? If so, can you compare what you read to how this person actually feels?

Practice Pointer

When you begin to pay attention to auras, make sure you have a strong sense of being grounded and secure. This way you will not absorb the energy that you are attempting to read.

Ask yourself whether you can tell by the color of the aura, by white or golden energy, by sound, by feeling, by touch, by smell, or by taste? Can you dowse the individual's energy field? Can you feel negative or positive energy, and how can you apply what you feel to the actual health of the person? How about taste and smell? At first, you may want to keep a record of your observations to help validate the information you are receiving.

Identify Healthy and Unhealthy Auras

The next step is to apply your knowledge of how you read an aura to how you can develop an understanding of what you are reading. As you get experience, you will notice aura patterns that can give a sense of what the auras mean. These patterns will help you produce mind models of what is a good positive healthy aura and a negative unhealthy one.

Healing the Source of Negative Energy

Once you have an understanding of positive and negative auras, you can begin to locate the specific areas of a person's body that emit negative energy. You may even be able to determine through your five senses what the cause of the negative energy is and develop a healing model for the negative aura. In other words, you may be able to diagnose what someone's negative aura means and then develop a model for her to change it if she chooses to.

There are two specific ways that healing energy is transferred through you. It either comes in through you, or you let it flow out through you into the Universe. If you are a receiver, you are on the receiving end of someone else's energy. This ability is enhanced by your mental makeup. Receivers who do not find an outlet for the energy they take in can take on the characteristics of that energy.

A Psychic Truth

Many people do not want to know anything that makes them feel responsible for someone else. They put up a defensive mental shield to block any such knowledge. If you have knowledge, don't expect others to accept what you know. All you can do is drop hints and hope they discover them.

If you do not understand your ability to receive energy, you can be overwhelmed by it when you begin to develop your psychic abilities of reading and working with auras. Massage students can suddenly manifest the pain that a client is feeling. A beginning Reiki student may feel the client's illness, whether mentally or physically. If you absorb the energy of the person you are trying to heal, that's because you haven't been able to work with your Belief System and have taken ownership of someone else's negative energy.

The other type of healer sends a strong Universal Energy through herself from an external source and into the client's body so that it flows over and removes the negative energy. The sender creates a stronger image of power, whereas the absorber is much more mellow. One potential problem for the projector is that the ego, and not the Universe, is responsible for the healing. If you take ownership of the power, you can totally change the healing energy into your own negative energy, which is not good for your clients or for you.

Develop a Model for Healing

What is going to be your strategy for healing? Can you develop a model in your mind of how you read someone's energy? Which of the senses or combination of senses will you use—vision, hearing, feeling, taste, or smell? Can you create a negative model and from that a positive model for a change? Can you imagine helping transform the negative aura into a positive aura? Your image would be based on the way you understand the difference between negative and positive auras.

Are you a sender or a receiver? Your conscious mind may not know yet, but your unconscious and your Universal Mind do. You may feel the Universal Power in your fingers, or you may have the ability to snatch away the negative aura and deposit it out in the vast Universe. You may want to take classes in alternative healing, such as Reiki, or in ways of understanding auras to help you find and develop your gifts.

Practice Pointer

Whenever you work on yourself or someone else with healing energy, remember you are only doing something that is complementary to Western medicine. You are not offering a substitute for what a medical doctor would do.

You can always practice on yourself. Try slowly smoothing out your own aura, especially on days when you feel out of balance. Can you create an image of any negative energy that might be in you? If so, can you bring a positive image over the negative and feel yourself being filled with universal peace and love from a healing energy at the same time? You may be amazed at the positive effect that healing energy can have on you or on someone else.

Harness the Power of Universal Force

Now it's time to focus on bringing the Universal Force through you as a healing energy. Try this with yourself first. When you work with others, you will not be able to put yourself in the same state of relaxation as you can when you are working with yourself. However, you will still be able to develop a strong connection to the Universal Power.

Take a deep breath and exhale slowly. Feel your body relaxing as you continue to breathe slowly in and out. When you are ready, focus on your third eye and let yourself feel the Universal Force of peaceful and loving healing energy begin to flow in through your third-eye chakra. You may feel this healing force as it starts to flow down through your body to your throat chakra. Let the healthy feeling of peace and love balance your throat center and continue on until all your energy centers are open and balanced with the peaceful and healing love of the Universal Force.

Feel your highest chakra, the crown center, open and balance, as you are aware of the total connection and protection of the Universal Force. You may ask your Belief that only the purest healing energy may flow through you to be passed on to the proper area of your or someone else's physical, mental, or spiritual body. You may ask that this loving healing energy allow the person for whom it is intended to find his or her balance and be tuned by this universal healing energy.

Let the Energy Flow

Now that you are centered, grounded, and protected by universal love, you may begin allowing the healing energy to flow through the areas that need healing. Remember, do it your way, the way that you have already identified as using your most powerful image senses. If you are clairvoyant, see. If you are clairaudient, hear. If you are clairsentient, feel.

If you are strong in taste and smell imagery, use those senses to help amplify the universal healing energy of peace and love that is flowing through you. If you are a receiver, ask for the negative energy to be collected by your loving hands so that it can be sent out into the Universe to be healed with peace and love. The more you practice these concepts, adding the special things that work only for you, you will find yourself more and more in tune with the healing, peaceful, and loving energy of the Universe.

Work with Someone Else

Once you are comfortable working with yourself, it is time to work with others. Use the knowledge that you have gained through your experiences, and work with someone you know who is receptive. Start slowly, and just read his aura so that you can develop a model of his health. Look for positive and negative energy and physical, mental, and spiritual balance.

Practice Pointer

It is very important to remember that you are not the healer—the Universe is. Your responsibility is to keep yourself in balance so that you are the best conduit possible for the universal healing energy.

When you have decided on a healing strategy, start to bring positive energy in and draw the negative energy out. This action is meant to help an individual connect to the universal healing energy. Always center yourself, and ask the Universal Mind to send its healing energy of love and peace either through you into the person or directly into the person. Next, you draw the negative energy out through you to flow back into the Universe to be healed with peace and love.

The Art of Reiki and Other Healing Methods

Healing may also be performed through a practice such as Reiki, massage, body scanning, or magnetic healing—some of the many alternative-healing methods available to you today.

The Art of Reiki

Reiki is an ancient healing practice that has undergone an impressive revival over the past few decades. After centuries of being forgotten, it was rediscovered in the 1800s by Dr. Mikao Usui, a Japanese scholar and physician who stumbled upon it while researching sacred texts on the healing methods of Jesus. Dr. Usui spent his life developing the method of Reiki and using it to heal the poor, as well as teaching the technique to a few of his disciples.

> A PSYCHIC TRUTH
>
> Reiki is the Universal Life Force. In Japanese, rei is the universal transcendental spirit and mysterious power, and ki is the vital life force. The energy in Reiki comes from the life force of the Universe.

Reiki attunes the energy centers in the body with the Universal Life Force. Its practitioners have specific hand positions that connect the energy with the client. They spend about five minutes in each position before moving to the next. At the same time, the practitioner may use his or her intuitive ability to help certain areas of the body to heal using the Life Force energy.

There are three degree levels in Reiki. Levels I and II are taught in a relatively short time span and can usually be completed within a weekend. Level III is the master level. Learning and practicing the beginning levels of Reiki is not very expensive, and it a good way to begin experiencing alternative modalities. The fee for completing the third degree can run as high as $10,000.

Massage Therapy

Another healing technique is good old massage, because it uses hands-on techniques for comfort and healing. There are many different kinds of massage therapies, such as Swedish massage, which is very popular in health clubs and spas. Many massage therapists use their psychic ability to work the part of their client's body that has an energy block. A sensitive, in-tune, balanced massage therapist can also perform very effective healing practices by combining her knowledge of the human body with her intuitive abilities.

Body Scanning

Some of you may actually be able to scan a human body in your mind and develop an image of the person's health by using your five different senses. A medical intuitive can psychically read your body and come up with a diagnosis in actual medical terms. Each intuitive will work differently, but they all have a common goal, namely, the wellness of their clients. If you have the ability to scan a human body in your mind, you may want to seek out some training in the medical field so that you can effectively communicate the images you psychically receive.

> ### A Psychic Truth
> Each individual's healing modality is often developed around the specific abilities of the founder. You will hear terms such as Universal Life Force, which may mean the same as Universal Force, and even the religious concepts of God. You will get to know these truths in your own way.

Magnetic Healing

The principle of magnetic healing has been used since Anton Mesmer worked with animal magnetism. He believed that he could rearrange invisible fluid in the body and bring about healing. Today there are magnets of different sizes that wearers believe can cure all kinds of ailments, such as lameness. There are magnetic bracelets and magnets to put in your shoes, and many people claim to be helped by wearing them.

Keep Your Wits about You!

Unfortunately, there are also people who claim to be psychic healers and yet have only a single true ability—the talent for scamming trusting and desperate people. These "psychic healers" have a bag of tricks, including incantations, to chase the illness out of the body and rituals to heal any affliction known. Of course, there is a hefty fee for their services.

To take it one step further, there are also "psychic surgeons." They do the surgery with their bare hands and are psychically able to plunge them into the body of their patient. They even pull out the bad body part and close the "wound" without a trace of a scar. They also have the ability to give "psychic injections" using their fingers as needles. Many of the body parts that have been analyzed after these so-called surgeries turned out to be organs from chickens.

However, there are many excellent psychics out there as well, and they may be exactly right for you. If you are looking for help from a psychic or from any other alternative healer, always ask what training they have had and how long they have been in practice. It is never a bad idea to ask for references from some of their colleagues. You may want to ask for a consultation first before deciding on the approach you want to take.

Your Own Medical Intuition

Do you know or think that you have a psychic gift to be a medical intuitive? If you have this ability, it does not mean that you have to announce it to everyone you know. Once you become aware of your potential, you are free to use it in your own best interests and those of others, in a way that is comfortable and positive for you. Here are some questions to help you identify your healing strengths.

Do you have intuitive feelings about your or other people's health? If so, how do you get these feelings? Can you intuit other people's medical problems? If so, how? Is it through mental pictures, or colors, or just energy? Do you hear voices or other sounds that indicate a medical problem? Do you get a feeling of health problems? If so, where do you feel it, mentally or physically? Can you touch and feel auras? Can you dowse a body for health problems?

Do you experience smells that indicate health situations? It might be in the smell of someone's breath or body odor. Do you get a taste in your mouth that might give you a clue to a health condition? You may even get combinations of sense images that can give you a clearer indication of your own or another person's health condition.

Using Your Psychic Ability

If you have the psychic gift of knowing health conditions of others, you may want to develop it further. A medical intuitive is someone who has the ability to read others' health conditions and translate them into traditional medical terms. The diagnosis can then be treated medically. As with body scanning, you may want to seek the proper medical training to help you communicate what you already know psychically.

Practice Pointer

If you want to develop your healing gifts, study as many alternative healing modalities as possible to help you decide which one works best for you and for those with whom you will work. The way you work with healing practices will be different from anyone else's way of working. The important thing is that whatever you do works best for yourself and others.

If you are already working in the medical field—whether as a doctor, a nurse, or in another professional capacity—and you have the psychic gift of reading health conditions, then you are ready to develop your intuitive side. The first step is to understand what you already know psychically. This includes understanding your mental makeup and learning how your mind processes sensory information. The next step is to create a plan to help you further sharpen your natural psychic talents. You are already in the health profession, so why not use all your tools and knowledge to help your patients heal?

Your Responsibility as a Healer

Not everyone is comfortable with the role of healer. It is a special gift, and it comes with a lot of responsibility. The first is to acknowledge that the real healer is the Universal Force of peace and love. The second is to understand that you are not a doctor or a nurse unless you are trained as one, and you are only assisting a person to use her mental and spiritual selves to work with those trained in medicine to bring about wellness. As a psychic healer, you are not a substitute for a trained medical professional.

Practice Pointer

It is very important to take care of yourself mentally, physically, and spiritually so that you will be in tune to work with the healing energy of the Universe. The opportunity you've been given is unique and different from anyone else's on earth. It is your choice to be in tune with it.

So many gifted psychics, whether they are healers or work in other modalities, do not live up to the responsibility of keeping themselves in balance. The result is the work they do may not be their best and they may not be able to use their intuitive healing gifts to the best of their potential.

11

Visiting a Psychic Reader or Medium

Have you ever gone to a psychic? Many people go, either for a specific reason or just for fun. Some believe what they're told, while others are too skeptical to believe anything. They allow their skepticism to block them from being open to the messages in the reading. It's possible that you've never visited a psychic but that you have called a psychic phone line. If so, what was the experience like?

People have many questions about the future, particularly in regard to their finances, career, and relationships. Many visit psychics in order to get good advice and some insights—in terms of the past and present as well as the future. There is also a great deal of interest in visiting a psychic medium to contact loved ones who have died. Some want to know whether their loved ones are all right and whether they are still out there someplace. Others want to finish some of their unresolved communication from when their loved ones were still alive. It is also possible for the deceased to pass on some insight pertaining to the future of the living.

A PSYCHIC TRUTH

You might wonder what the difference between a psychic reader and a medium is. Well, a medium is a person who has the ability to communicate with the dead, and not all psychics have this ability. In other words, mediums are psychic, but not all psychics are mediums.

If you are planning to visit a psychic for a specific reason, you may want to do some homework before you make an appointment. Many psychics have a specialty and are much more accurate within their particular area of expertise, like past lives, health issues, or relationship situations.

If you decide to visit a psychic on a whim—for no apparent reason at all, and with no specific agenda—you may be more open to the messages that you are given during the session. It's also possible that your own psychic intuition will guide you to a particular psychic for a specific reason that you are not consciously aware of.

Being Skeptical

It's okay to be skeptical about visiting a psychic. If you are a pessimist, you will probably wonder if psychics can be relied on to tell the truth—after all, you may think, they are just giving the clients what they want to hear. If you feel uncomfortable about visiting a psychic, you are certainly under no obligation to do it.

However, you can avoid quacks and charlatans and find a psychic who is right for you, as long as you keep your eyes open. Be wary of psychics who are concerned about money and suggest various services they insist you need. It's okay to look for ulterior motives when visiting a psychic you don't know.

You also need to be aware of the fact that every psychic will vary in accuracy. In fact, if you went to a single psychic over a period of time, you might get a difference in the quality and accuracy of your readings. On certain days your psychic may be out of balance and unable to give a true reading. Or, it may be that you aren't as open at one time as you are at another.

You won't always know where the interferences are coming from. For example, when the psychic Edgar Cayce went to Texas in search of oil, it seemed as though every step of the way something went wrong, and he failed to locate the "mother lode." Even though Cayce believed that he was doing it for the good of his work, it turned out that other partners in the company had other intentions for the profits. Because their intentions were not in keeping with Cayce's work, his energy was blocked and he was unable to gain the psychic balance and discover the oil.

Your First Psychic Visit

When you visit a psychic, it is good to remember that you have purchased a service. It is your right to receive your money's worth. It is always easy to become emotionally wrapped up. Your emotions, however, can distort your impartial view of the reading procedure. The following are some questions to ask yourself that may help you judge what is happening.

1. Is the psychic trying to intimidate or confuse you with her appearance or the surroundings for the reading?

2. Is there an opportunity or an attempt to gain information about you that could be used in your reading? Is there anything that the psychic does during the reading that indicates that she is looking for information to feed back to you?

3. Does the psychic seek to get confidential information from or about you, such as your financial situation or home address?

4. Will the psychic allow you to make a tape recording or video of your reading?

5. Does the psychic try to sell you other services or get you to come back for more appointments?

6. Is the psychic positive, and does she provide a potential for improvement in your life? Or is she negative, quick with warnings of doom and gloom?

Practice Pointer

Before your appointment to get a psychic reading, prepare by centering yourself. It is necessary for you to have positive intentions. If you go with a closed mind, it could prove to be frustrating for both you and the psychic.

A Cold Reading

The first time you visit a psychic, you will get what is known as a cold reading—a reading made for someone the psychic has never met. This type of reading is different from one in which there may have been previous contact or in which the psychic was privy to a certain amount of information about you. It is not uncommon for someone who has a favorite psychic to visit him periodically over a span of time. In such a case, the psychic becomes familiar with many aspects of that client's life.

A cold reading is a good way to see if the psychic knows his stuff. For you to have confidence in the reading, he will need to give you some information that proves to you that he is "right on." This material may not have anything to do with why you went for a reading, but at the same time it does validate certain information that you know that the psychic could not have known before you met.

Don't Give Any Clues

Be aware that some psychics are very skilled at eliciting information from you without your awareness. They are experts in observation. Every movement of your body, eyes, and facial muscles provides clues. The sound of your voice can verify whether the information they just gave you created an emotional reaction. Even the slightest hesitation can provide instant information.

To get information, a psychic may start off with general statements/questions. As you agree or disagree, the psychic develops a general profile of you in her mind. For example, she may say something like, "I see that you have had some sadness in your life, wouldn't you agree?" When you answer that question, you are bound to give the psychic some information about yourself that will lead her to another question.

Practice Pointer

When you visit a psychic for the first time, be aware of the clothes and jewelry you are wearing. If you bring someone with you and you have to wait for your reading, make sure you do not discuss the reason you are there.

This technique is no different than what a good salesman would use when convincing you to buy his product. He'll first find out what you are looking for and then will describe his product with those same words. In this case, the psychic is looking for clues about you and your problem. Be sure you recognize this approach—this is not how psychic work should be done.

Psychic Validations

What the psychic may start out with is psychic validation—stepping into your energy information flow to retrieve information about you or others in your life, either current or past. This process serves two purposes. The psychic is validating to you that she is receiving accurate information that is already known to you but could not be known to the psychic. Additionally, this information acts as sort of a "pump primer" for the psychic.

During the validation process, the psychic is getting deeper into the "zone." Just as you practiced deepening exercises in earlier chapters, the psychic focuses on the source of knowledge that currently relates to you. It is impossible to hold that focus for a long period of time, so the psychic may drift in and out of the zone throughout the reading. You will get the best information when the psychic is in the zone.

Gathering Your Thoughts about Group Readings

Another popular type of reading is a group reading. The size of the group may vary from a few people to an audience in a theater. As the psychic makes his entrance, he begins to pull information from his Source about the people present at the reading. Some psychics use special effects, such as lighting, music, or meditation to help both themselves and the listeners enter the right state for the readings. They may also use certain rituals or routines to help induce a receptive trance state.

The group reading may have several different parts, including a message of wisdom from the guides or the Universe, a time for random readings focused on the audience, and a time for questions and answers. You may be selected, and you may not be. It's all up to the Universe—or is it?

Practice Pointer

It is natural to want to go out and take immediate action based on your new insights. It may be better, however, to let the dust settle. You might sleep on it and let your intuition digest it for you. Any immediate concerns can be given to your Belief System to help define an action.

Many of the same cautions for a private session are also true for a group session. Was there a possibility that presession chatter was overheard? Were there other opportunities in which information could have been extracted without the participants knowing? Did the guests reveal too much personal information? Can you observe how the psychic may be gathering material in a nonpsychic manner?

Go with the Flow

One of the best things you can do when you go to a group reading is to relax and go with the flow. If you are overanxious for information, you may telegraph that desire to the psychic, who in return may feed you back the same bits and pieces that you have already given him.

Long-Distance Readings Can Work, Too

It is not necessary to be in the presence of a psychic in order to receive a valid reading. As far back as the early 1900s, Edgar Cayce would respond to letters requesting readings. He traveled in his mind to the physical location of the subject and could give details such as the current weather. Toward the end of his life, his abilities to give readings over long distances were so well known that he was besieged with far more requests than he could fulfill.

When the use of the telephone became widespread, it became possible to give live psychic consultation from a great distance. Then came live call-in radio shows. Later, television shows allowed psychics to share their readings and advice with many listeners at the same time. (This also helped to popularize the leading psychics.)

Today, the Internet is a resource that enables you to contact psychics from all over the world. Many have books and other products for sale as well as online readings. It is possible to correspond with some of them before paying for anything. Let your own intuition be your guide if you decide to check out online psychics.

The Truth about Predictions

Are psychic predictions "cast in stone"? What do you think? If you are told something about an event that is going to happen, how will that affect your life? Is it possible to make changes that avoid predicted outcomes?

The concept of time is complicated enough to fill dozens of books. But what you need to understand when it comes to psychic readings is that a psychic prediction is based on images of the future as they are influenced by the events of yesterday and today. If nothing changes in the progression that leads into the future, the prediction has a good chance of coming true. However, if something happens to change the normal progression of events, the prediction will no longer be valid.

It is always good to watch out for potential agenda issues that a psychic may or may not have. Pay attention to your own psychic intuition. Remember, you can take steps to change the prediction. The event is still in the future. You might consider a lifestyle change, eating or other habit change, or change of travel dates.

A Psychic Truth

Fear of the future can paralyze you in the moment, keeping you captive and holding you from moving into the unknown. You don't need to take the risk by yourself. If you rely on your guide, you may have the courage to move forward, one step at a time.

Dealing with the Future

When you receive information about your future, whether it's good news or bad, the first step in dealing with it is to make sure that you are grounded in the present. Use your ability to connect to your third eye and your inner guidance system. Ask yourself what is the best way to work with the knowledge that you have been given in a good and positive way. You can even ask for the right words to come out of your mouth and for the right actions to be taken.

Next, ask your inner guidance system for some verification of the action that may be required. You may have already heard the message before. Ask for protection from the Golden Light of the Universe. Above all, listen to the messages that are coming through you internally and given to you externally. It's okay to use your own guidance system.

You may want to use your ability to contact your inner guidance system regarding future potential events. The methods that you have had a chance to experience in earlier chapters can be very effective in helping you deal with possible anxieties concerning the future. The reality of life is what is happening at the moment, and each moment can have an impact on the future, either positively or negatively.

Psychic Power: A Gift or a Curse?

As you have already discovered by examining your mental makeup, every person is different, and the same truth applies to psychics. Some psychics see their abilities as a service that should be paid for.

Others refuse to charge money, believing that their gift is something to share freely. This is true not only in intuitive areas, but also in many other creative fields such as art, music, and writing.

A Psychic Truth

Many gifted psychics have not had easy lives. For many, the intuitive gift is also a curse. It's difficult to face your own health, financial, or relationship issues. Even Edgar Cayce did not listen to the advice of a reading that was given about his own health.

You may be just as psychic as the psychic whom you visit to get a reading. The only difference is that you may not have identified your gifts yet. It does take courage to take the first step in giving yourself permission to understand that you are psychic. Now that you have almost finished this book, you may be starting to recognize and understand your intuitive gifts and ready to take that big step of beginning to help others.

As you examine how some of the gifted readers do it, you may discover a method or area that you can use as a model to develop your special type of psychic ability. In the previous chapters, you investigated different types of psychic abilities. You may have found some that work for you, and some that do not.

12

Continuing Development

You have now had a chance to learn about and try many different psychic techniques. You have been shown how to identify and understand the intuitive gifts that you were born with and that you may already have been using throughout your life. You have developed ways to be in tune with your internal and external guidance systems. You may have been able to meet and identify your guides, angels, or other spirits that are there to help guide and protect you. You have also learned about the importance of staying grounded in the universal light.

You know of the possibility that you have a soul map to follow for growth during this lifetime, and you can now work with your Belief System. You have had a chance to compare yourself to the pros, and you have found that maybe your psychic ability is as good as theirs. Finally, you have had the opportunity to try and to experiment with many different types of psychic techniques and tools. By now, I hope, you have a good basic concept of your psychic strengths.

Staying on Course

Your next step is to decide what to do to continue your psychic development. The goal of this book is to help you identify your intuitive strengths. Now that you have had that chance, you have a wonderful opportunity to become in tune with your life map and your soul's journey. It is time to decide how you will put your psychic abilities to work. After all, it is part of your life plan.

You have probably been focusing your unconscious and your Universal Mind on the lesson of each chapter as you have gone through this book. Now focus on your internal and external guidance systems to let your psychic abilities become in tune with your life purpose.

An Exercise to Help You Find the Way

You can use your basic self-hypnosis technique to work with your unconscious and your Universal Mind to help determine the direction your psychic gifts will take. Find your comfortable place, loosen your clothes, take a deep breath, exhale, and relax. Focus on your third eye and let your eyes close. Continue breathing in and out slowly while you begin to work your way down through your chakras, opening and balancing each one until you return to your crown chakra. Now focus on the Universal Energy of peace and love as you begin to surround yourself with the Golden Light of the Universe. You may feel it wrapping around you like a protective bubble of golden love and peace.

When you are ready, slowly count yourself down from five to zero, focusing more and more on your connection to your Belief and your guides or angels. Use your self-hypnosis anchors to help deepen your trance and strengthen your connection to the Universal Mind. When you arrive at zero, take some time to reflect and enjoy the loving and peaceful energy of your universal connection.

Connect to Your Belief

Now ask your Belief to help you determine the way your psychic gifts should be used to benefit mankind. You may ask your guides or angels or other spirits to communicate with you in a way that you will recognize and understand. Ask that you may use this information to help you become in tune with your life map. Now give yourself a little time to be open for guidance and then suggest that after you count yourself back up to five that you will remain open to the messages and guidance from the Universe.

Practice Pointer

Once you have counted yourself back to five and have come back to the surface of your mind, you can prepare yourself for guidance from your inner and outer team. As you have learned, that guidance may manifest itself in many different ways. It may come from inside yourself or from something you hear from someone else. You may hear it more than once.

If You Call Yourself a Psychic . . .

You can now call yourself a psychic. You have the unlimited power of the Universe at the tip of your third eye. All you have to do is shift your focus, and you are in instant contact. It can be very tempting to put this power to use for personal gain.

So, what are you going to do with your new knowledge? Are you planning to use it for personal gain? Are you tempted to reach out for the riches and prosperity that you might have once thought were rightfully yours? Do you want to be able to gain an advantage over others so that you can manipulate and control them?

Yes, you can use your psychic abilities for personal gain, but for how long? Free will is your opportunity to go your own way instead of in the direction of your soul's journey. Remember what karma is. Are you willing to risk your investment in the future growth of your soul for momentary personal gain to satisfy your ego?

Prepare Physically

Part of your obligation is to keep yourself in tune physically for your psychic journey. If you are able, it is important that you find the time to stay as fit as possible. That means getting the right exercise and making the proper choice of healthful foods. The more you keep your physical body in condition to be a conduit for psychic energy, the better your connection to the Universal Mind will be. Your physical condition is a part of your psychic development.

PRActice POinteR

You have an inner guidance system that will let you know if you are going in a direction that is not in tune with your life journey. Pay attention to your warning system and take the time to get refocused on your life purpose.

Prepare Mentally

It is also important for you to keep yourself in as good a mental condition as possible for your upcoming psychic journey. Remember to keep a healthy mental perspective. Take the time to use your relaxation exercises to help keep your psychic energy in balance. Also use your mental anchors to trigger relaxed states during times when it is hard to escape the stresses that you encounter. The more time you can spend in a positive waking trance state, the more you will be mentally in tune with your psychic development.

Prepare Spiritually

The more grounded and comfortable you are with your personal belief, the more in tune with your spirituality you will be. Make sure that you are in touch many times a day with your spirit guides, your angels, or whatever you believe is there to help guide you on your soul's journey. The more you are open to your internal and external guidance systems, the more you will learn to rely on the power and strength of the Universal Energy. Remember always to be aware of keeping your chakra centers balanced and open to the peace and love of the Universe and to keep grounded in universal golden light.

Practice Your Talent

Just as with any other talent, if you do not use your psychic talent it will eventually dwindle away. Now that you have identified your psychic gifts, it is time for you to work with them on a steady basis. You may have more than one area that you want to develop. Make sure that you develop a plan that is workable for you. Many times people get very excited at learning something new at first, but if they do not quickly establish a routine, they can easily lose interest and abandon their project.

Set aside a period of time everyday to work with your psychic ability. It doesn't have to be long, perhaps as little as fifteen minutes to start—the time you will need to take will depend on what you are working on and the potential need for companions in your work (whether you need to be alone, near people, or actually work with others). If you are using a self-hypnotic trance, you will not want to be interrupted. If you are reading people or energies, you will want to be in a place where you have access to different subjects.

Practice Pointer

Pay attention to how your psychic development is affecting you. When you remain focused on it for a period of time, are you able to clear it from your mind after you have finished a session? Are you able to sleep peacefully, or do you toss and turn?

Be aware that you may meet some resistance from other people, family, or friends. They may resent that you are spending time away from them. They may not believe in psychic abilities and may not be happy that you have that gift. They may not want you to mention the subject anywhere around them. You may have to find a way to balance your psychic development and your family and friends.

Break Up Energy Buildup

One of the hazards that you may face as you become more and more in tune with your intuitive abilities is psychic energy buildup. What this means is that when you take a large amount of Universal Energy into your body, it is possible to build up a surplus. If it does not find an outlet, it will manifest itself in different ways, such as with an intense electrical tingling. As an example, if you are using your hands for healing and are bringing in the energy for that purpose, it is possible that you feel prickly sensations in your hands.

It is always a good idea when you are working with energy to keep yourself grounded. There are several ways to do this. If the energy surplus is localized, such as in your hands or feet, the easy way is to touch the ground with the parts of your body that are overcharged. You can also shake your hands, your arms, or your fingers to help disperse the energy back into the Universe. Deep breathing is another excellent way as long as you let the energy flow out of your body when you exhale. If your entire body feels like it has been charged, you may want to exercise, go for a walk, or swim to help dissipate energy.

Washing your hands and arms in cold water, bathing your feet, or immersing your whole self are all good ways to get rid of surplus energy. Remember that this charged energy is a healing energy and you can feel a sense of universal peace and health as you let it flow back out into the Universe. The goal is to keep yourself in balance and in tune so that you retain the proper amount of healing and psychic energy.

Remember Where Your Power Originates

Another problem many novice psychics face is learning to develop and use their psychic abilities while keeping in mind where the source of their power and knowledge originates. As you continue working on developing your psychic abilities, continually ask yourself where your powers are coming from. Are they there for your responsible use and for the good of all? Or do you have the right to claim it as your own and use it for your personal short-term goals?

A Psychic Truth

Develop a positive belief habit as you progress in your psychic growth. The more you give acknowledgment to your Belief and your guidance systems, the easier it will be to avoid the problems of the ego and the conflict of ownership. This will free you up to stay in proper focus.

Owning something implies a certain amount of responsibility. If you impress on others that you have a psychic power, you will be expected to live up to your ability.

Unfortunately your psychic power may not turn on and off like a light switch. Every time you receive psychic energy it may be a little different. Your connection to the Universe can sometimes be very strong and at other times very weak. Your job is to be ready to experience it when it is called for. The more you practice, the stronger your psychic connection will become.

If you take all the credit, then you will have to accept the failures that are bound to happen. If you acknowledge the ownership of the Universe, then there are no failures, only honest attempts to succeed. Once you have established clear universal ownership of your psychic abilities, not only in your mind but also in the minds of others, you will have the freedom to let it flow without the pressure to turn it on and perform.

"I" or "Eye"?

The words you use to describe your psychic abilities and who owns them will either give you the freedom to experience or commit you to success or failure. When you say, "I have a psychic power," are you talking about yourself or the Universe?

It is okay to use the word as long as you mean your third eye or your universal connection. The Universe has incredible power as long as you accept what it has to offer. If you claim that it is yours instead, will you be able to handle the responsibility?

When you relate your third "eye" to your excitement over your psychic development, you can keep a balance with your ego "I." Whenever you are aware that you are having a psychic insight, remember to focus on your third eye for a brief moment and give thanks to the Universe for the miracle of knowing. When the insights are very good and you receive praise for your work, you can say "thank you" graciously and tell the person praising you that you will pass the message on to the true provider of your psychic information. At the same time you can feel the peace and love of the Universe radiating through you. Use this feeling as an anchor to your Belief.

It's Okay to Be Excited

It is okay to be excited over the discovery and development of your psychic gifts. It can be an amazing process. Every day can be a new adventure of learning and personal growth. However, don't expect that everyone else will be as excited about your intuitive development as you are. As long as you are bringing positive Universal Energy of peace and love, each person you connect with will have the opportunity to benefit from your enthusiasm. Focus your excitement onto the incredible power of the Universe, and remember to keep yourself in balance with it.

One Step at a Time

However, it is very easy to become so wrapped up in your new psychic adventure that it becomes the center of your focus. For a period of time you may not think of anything else. It may be in your mind every waking moment, and you may dream about it at night. You may grow to resent any outside interference that keeps you from immersing yourself in your psychic development.

> ### A Psychic Truth
> As you grow in your psychic ability, you may not think the way you did before you started. This is because your sense imagery has developed, and you are in a state of change. You may feel distanced from those whom you used to be close to.

It is important to be able to find a balance between your psychic development and the rest of your world. Regardless of the transformation you are going through, you still need to be aware of family relationships and your work and other commitments. It is very possible that you will grow spiritually and find yourself out of place with many of your old friends and things you used to do. You may not be able to explain your new knowledge to others, no matter how hard you try.

If you try to progress faster than you should, you will become out of tune with your purpose. You may open up to more psychic energy than you bargained for. Remember to make sure that your chakras are always in balance and that your energy flow is positive. After all, you are only a part of a grand universal scheme that will unfold in its own way.

Trust Your Teachers to Appear When You Need Them

Always continue to be a student of the Universe. There is so much more that you can learn as you follow your soul's journey. Your teachers will appear when you are ready for the lesson. They may come at any time and from anywhere, while you are asleep, as an inner voice, or from someone you know or may have just met. Study, read, listen, and try out techniques to gain further knowledge.

Here are some suggestions to help you find support in your psychic journey:

1. Find or start a metaphysical discussion group in your area.

2. Use the Internet to develop positive metaphysical contacts.

3. Take a course in psychic development at a school such as Atlantic University.

4. Find a friend with similar interests.

5. Ask your Belief to help you connect with the right resources for your psychic development.

How Does It Fit?

Whenever you investigate new knowledge and skills that can enhance your abilities, it is good to always ask yourself how someone else's philosophies or techniques fit you. How do their ideas compare with how you believe?

What is right for someone else may not be right for your psychic development. Remember that you are the one who intuitively knows whether or not a piece of information fits into your life map.

Along the Road, on Your Life Path

Our society teaches that you should always strive for personal gain and achievement. Many of the people who make this view their focus wind up at the end of their life journeys feeling a lack of a total fulfillment, regardless of their personal gains or the accumulation of wealth. On the way to reaching their personal goals, they have missed their soul's potential growth. They let their free will make the choices that put them out of touch with their life map.

Practice Pointer

As you near the completion of this book, now is an excellent time to use your communication with your guidance systems to help assess where you are in your life journey. How do you feel about your soul's journey? What can you do next to help stay on course?

It is very easy to feel inadequate and to develop low self-esteem when others flaunt their personal achievements in front of you. You may feel you have nothing to offer that will compare. You may have brought with you a past-life feeling that your personal gains are all that matters in life. You may be pushed by friends or family members to match the achievements of others whom you know. You may be open to ridicule and considered a failure if you do not meet their standards of success.

If you approach your life journey as a battlefield where the domineering force rules, you will always be in inner conflict. If you work with your guidance teams and believe that the result of your work will be in the best interests of all concerned, you will be opening your psychic abilities to help keep you in tune with your soul's potential growth. Your life need not seem as if it were a battlefield but can be instead a great adventure into the unknown. Every day can bring with it the potentials for amazing revelations.

It takes courage to take the risk and trust in your Belief to go against the flow. It is okay to know what others around you may not. Once you understand that you have access to the secrets of the Universe, you can feel free to use this knowledge to help others if they choose to allow themselves to learn. Remember, you are only a piece of the Universe, and your job is to focus on your assignment. The Universe will take care of everything else.

Practice Pointer

Proceed slowly! It is always very tempting to go as fast as you can once you have an idea of what your life potential might be. Remember that you are only one piece of the universal puzzle. If you are open to your assignments, you will go at the correct speed.

When you give someone a gift, you usually pick out something that you feel will be good for that person. If the recipient rejects it, you will probably be disappointed. The reality is that once they own the gift, they can do with it whatever they want. When you offer intuitive wisdom to someone, remember that it is no different from a physical gift that they can accept or reject. It is their choice, not yours.

This Is Just the Beginning—Enjoy Your Journey!

It is time for you to begin the incredible journey that lies ahead of you. You now have the knowledge and the tools to help you become in tune with your life purpose. You may want to refer to certain sections of this book until you feel confident and grounded in your Belief System. Remember that you may adapt any of the views stated here to fit how you intuitively feel. It is the purpose and significance of your journey that is important, not the attempt to take an approach that does not feel right for you.

A PSYCHIC TRUTH

You have a life purpose and your psychic ability is a major part of it. If you accept the opportunity that you are offered, you may never view the world in the same way again. It may become rich in meaning and mystery and full of constant discovery.

Your friends, family, and coworkers may see something in you that they did not notice before. You may find that complete strangers are drawn to have a conversation with you. Every day you may notice miracles that have always existed around you but that you failed to see before. Life has the potential of taking on a completely new and exciting adventure for you. There is no way that you can successfully explain the incredible feeling of being in tune with your life map.

This book has within its covers a piece of your life map that is waiting for you to use to help you on your soul's journey. Your guides, angels, or spirits and the Universe have sent it to you. Every reader has been sent one. Have you discovered yours yet? Only you can recognize it. It is something that can help you rediscover and develop your psychic abilities that are a part of your soul's rich heritage. If you haven't discovered it yet, don't worry. It will be revealed to you when it is time for you to understand it if you so choose. Just be aware, go forward, and believe in your psychic gifts.

Appendix A

Akashic Book of Records: *A mythological book that contains detailed records of every soul's existence.*

anchor: *A physical or nonphysical reminder that recreates a previous emotional state.*

angel: *A positive entity whose purpose is to help you. In Christianity, a messenger of God.*

astral plane: *An experience of being outside of your physical body. An astral plane is not of the earth's plane.*

astral projection: *When a person leaves the physical body and travels to other places in or out of the earth's plane.*

astrology: *A system of predicting future events through studying the movement of celestial bodies.*

aura: *The energy field around a person or object.*

automatic writing: *Writing that comes from your unconscious mind while you're in a light trance state.*

bobber: *A tool used for dowsing.*

body scanning: *The ability to look psychically into and around a human body for the purpose of determining the subject's health. Body scanning can be experienced through any of the five different senses.*

chakras: *The body's energy centers.*

channel: *A conduit for something to pass through. A psychic channel is a person who has another spirit or entity communicate through her.*

clairaudience: *The gathering of information through the hearing sense.*

clairsentience: *The gathering of information through the sense of feeling.*

174

clairvoyance: *The gathering of information psychically through the visual sense.*

comfort zone: *A place or state of mind where you feel safe and little or no anxiety.*

conscious mind: *The surface of the mind; the communication center where you process thoughts and ideas.*

deductive psychic image: *A psychic image that comes from your* **unconscious mind***'s ability to take in external sensory stimuli.*

déjà vu: *The feeling that you have been someplace or done something before.*

diamons: *Divine spirits that offer wisdom, usually through internal voices.*

divination: *The ability to predict the future or find objects by information gathered through psychic abilities. Many different tools can be used to aid in divination.*

dowser: *A person who uses a psychic tool to locate underground water, mineral deposits, or other unseen things.*

dowsing: *A method of finding water or objects using psychic tools.*

exorcism: *A rite to get rid of evil spirits, usually performed by a priest.*

fairy: *A form of spirit resembling a small person; fairies are said to have magical powers.*

free will: *The freedom to choose—to follow or reject the soul's purpose.*

gatekeeper: *A strong and powerful guide who acts as your protector.*

glyph: *A horoscope symbol for each sun and moon sign.*

goal-focused psychic intuition: *A combination of deductive and random intuition.*

guidance system: *The guidance system has two parts; internal and external. Your internal guidance system is the connection to and advice from whatever it is you believe in—God, angels, guides, or other beings. Your external guidance system is made up of the elements that go with you to help you on your soul's journey.*

hologram: *A three-dimensional image.*

horoscope: *A chart developed from your birth date that includes the patterns of the heavens at the exact time of your birth. Your personal horoscope is meant to be your guide to the future, providing predictions of what might happen.*

hypnosis: *An altered state of consciousness in which the unconscious mind accepts suggestions.*

intuition: *The ability to know things that is not related to conscious reasoning.*

karma: *Unresolved situations from past lives that carry over into the current life.*

kinesthetic: *Sense of touch or feeling.*

life map: *Potential conditions for soul development that each person is born with; their* **free will** *to make life choices determines whether they will meet their potential.*

life work: *The plan for your soul's development during your present lifetime.*

L-rod: *A tool for* **dowsing** *that consists of two metal rods bent at a right angle and that swing easily with the use of tubes placed over the short ends.*

lucid dream: *A dream that starts in your dream state and continues into your waking state.*

magnetism: *Power that can bring about healing without using traditional medicine.*

Major Arcana: *The twenty-two cards that do not belong to one of the four suits of cards in the* **Tarot***. Each card has a specific theme and represents archetypal or major forces in your life.*

manifest reality: *Everything that can be touched or seen or heard or smelled or tasted.*

medical intuition: *The psychic gift of knowing the health condition of others.*

medium: *A person through whom the deceased can communicate with the living.*

mental telepathy: *Nonverbal communication through the mind.*

Minor Arcana: *Cards belonging to the four suits in the* **Tarot** *that represent four seasons, the directions, the elements, the four parts of your body, and the physical, mental, spiritual, and emotional. They are meant to help you focus on your direction in your life journey.*

miracle: *An occurrence with no explanation based on reality, usually attributed to a supernatural power that intervenes in the normal course of events.*

near-death experience: *A form of* **out-of-body experience**.

neurolinguistic programming (NLP): *A communication technique developed by Grinder and Bandler to change and improve thinking processes.*

open channel: *An altered state of consciousness in which you are open to the information flow and energies of other entities.*

Ouija board: *A board game that is designed to ask questions of spirits, who can answer with a "yes," "no," or by spelling out answers.*

out-of-body experience: *When energy leaves your body and goes someplace else.*

palmistry: *The ability to read the future by studying the lines and shapes of the palm of the hand.*

pendulum: *A tool for dowsing that consists of a string or chain with a weight at the end.*

phobia: *An anxiety disorder that is usually a fear of certain situations or specific objects.*

postcognition: *A visual image that shows how an event from the past actually happened.*

posthypnotic suggestion: *A suggestion given during a* **hypnosis trance** *that continues after the trance has ended.*

power animal: *A spirit animal that acts as a guide.*

precognition: *The knowledge of something that may happen in the future.*

premonition: *The feeling that something is going to happen before it does.*

psychic: *The ability to obtain information from sources that have no scientifically proven basis, such as intuition or the supernatural.*

psychokinesis: *The ability to levitate, move objects, heal, and manipulate psychic energy.*

quatrain: *Poetry form in which each stanza consists of four lines and rhymes alternately.*

random psychic intuition: *A psychic experience that comes at a time when it is unexpected and usually unwanted.*

reframe: *The installation of a new habit into the* **unconscious mind**.

Reiki: *A practice of transferring healing energy from the Universal Life Force through the practitioner to the subject. Dr. Mikao Usui developed this practice in the late 1800s.*

remote viewing: *A form of* **astral projection** *in which the subject is psychically able to view a specific location and to report what he or she observes.*

retrocognition: *Psychic information gathered from the past.*

rune: *A letter of the ancient alphabet used by Germanic peoples from approximately* A.D. *200 to 1200.*

Sanskrit: *The ancient language of the Hindu people of India.*

script: *The words used to help induce, deepen, and bring about a specific goal in a state of* **hypnosis.**

scrying: *Using visual aids to help produce the proper* **trance** *to see into the future.*

shaman: *A tribal medicine man, priest, or sorcerer.*

spirit: *A nonphysical entity.*

subconscious: *See* **unconscious mind.**

synchronicity: *More than one thing that happens at the same time.*

Tarot: *A deck of cards designed for psychic purposes—to help interpret past, present, and future events.*

telekinesis: *The ability to get a psychic image from an object by touching it.*

telepathy: *Communication of one mind with another by some means beyond normal sensory perception.*

teleportation: *The mental movement of objects over a distance.*

third eye: *The center of the forehead, which may feel tight and swollen by strong emotions and through which many believe the* **Universal Mind** *is contacted.*

time bending: *Merging different time periods for the purpose of healing the past.*

trance: *An altered state of consciousness in which the* **unconscious mind** *is open to suggestion and loses its ability to make critical decisions.*

unconscious mind: *The storage area of the mind that contains all your past experiences; also referred to as the* **subconscious**.

Universal Energy: *A form of energy that comes from your Belief System.*

Universal Flow: *The energy that is transmitted to and through you by the Universe or your Belief System.*

Universal Mind: *The part of your soul where you enlist the unknown to give you strength and produce miracles. See* **universal unconscious.**

universal unconscious: *Reached through the* **unconscious mind** *and believed to be the source from which you retrieve information and answers that have no scientific explanation; your Belief System.*

unmanifest reality: *Something real that cannot be seen or touched or readily explained.*

Appendix B

Further Reading

Ackerman, Diane, *The Natural History of the Senses* (New York: Random House, 1990).

Alexander, Skye. *The Everything® Tarot Book, 2ⁿᵈ Edition* (Avon, MA: Adams Media, 2006).

Besant, Annie, *A Study in Karma* (Adyar, Madras, India: Vasanta Press, 1987).

Brennan, Barbara Ann, *Hands of Light: A Guide to Healing Through the Human Energy Field* (New York: Bantam Books, 1988).

Browne, Sylvia, *Astrology Through a Psychic's Eyes* (Carlsbad, CA: Hay House, Inc., 2000).

DeBecker, Gavin, *The Gift of Fear: Survival Signals That Protect Us from Violence* (New York: Little, Brown & Company, 1997).

Ford, Arthur A., *A World Beyond* (Colorado Springs, CO: Fawcett Books, 1989).

Guiley, Rosemary Ellen, *Harper's Encyclopedia of Mystical & Paranormal Experience* (San Francisco: HarperSanFrancisco, 1991).

Hathaway, Michael R., *The Everything® Hypnosis Book* (Avon, MA: Adams Media, 2003).

Horan, Paula, *Empowerment Through Reiki* (Wilmot, WI: Lotus Light Publications, 1992).

Kirkpatrick, Sidney D., *Edgar Cayce: An American Prophet* (New York: Riverhead Books, 2000).

Kosarin, Jenni, *The Everything® Astrology Book, 2ⁿᵈ Edition* (Avon, MA: Adams Media, 2005).

———, *The Everything® Dreams Book, 2ⁿᵈ Edition* (Avon, MA: Adams Media, 2005).

Legge, James, *I Ching: Book of Changes* (New York: Bantam Books, 1977).

Moody, Raymond A., Jr., *Life after Life* (New York: Bantam Books, 1975).

Ridall, Kathryn, *Channeling: How to Reach Out to Your Spirit Guides* (New York: Bantam Books, 1988).

Roberts, Jane, *The Seth Material* (Englewood Cliffs, NJ: Prentice-Hall, Inc., 1970).

Stearn, Jess, *The Search for a Soul: Taylor Caldwell's Past Lives* (New York: Berkley Books, 1994).

Tyson, Donald, *Scrying for Beginners: Tapping into the Supersensory Powers of Your Subconscious* (St. Paul, MN: Llewellyn Publications, 2000).

Washington, Peter, *Madame Blavatsky's Baboon: A History of the Mystics, Mediums, and Misfits Who Brought Spiritualism to America* (New York: Schocken Books, 1995).

Woods, Walt, *Letter to Robin: A Mini-Course in Pendulum Dowsing* (Oroville, CA: The Print Shoppe, 2001).

Web Sites

Association for Research & Enlightenment: *www.edgarcayce.org*

Association for the Study of Dreams: *www.asdreams.org*

Astrology on the Web: *www.astrology.com*

Atlantic University (graduate program in transpersonal studies): *www.atlanticuniv.edu*

Chakra: *www.spiritweb.org*

Dowsers, American Society: *www.dowsers.org*

Edgar Cayce Foundation: *www.edgarcayce.org*

Hathaway, Michael R. (author of this book): *www.whitemountainhypnosiscenter.com*

International Center for Reiki Training: *www.reiki.org*

The International Society of Tarot: *www.tarotsociety.org*

John Edward—the Official John Edward Web site: *www.johnedward.net*

Light of the Soul—Links to Mediums: *www.lightofthesoul.net*

Lundegaard, Karen (medium): *www.karenlundegaard.com*

National Guild of Hypnotists: *www.ngh.net*

National Spiritualist Association of Churches: *www.nsac.org*

Parapsychology Foundation, Inc.: *www.parapsychology.org*

Séance.com: *www.theseance.com*

Van Praagh, James (medium): *www.vanpraagh.com*

Yoga Network: *www.yoganetwork.org*